THE *Astronomy* HANDBOOK

WILLIAM POTTER

SAFETY FIRST
Always tell an adult when you are intending to go outside and look at the stars, even if you are just at home.

This edition published in 2025 by Arcturus Publishing Limited
26/27 Bickels Yard, 151-153 Bermondsey Street,
London SE1 3HA

Copyright © Arcturus Holdings Limited

All rights reserved. No part of this publication may be reproduced, stored in a retrieval system, or transmitted, in any form or by any means, electronic, mechanical, photocopying, recording or otherwise, without prior written permission in accordance with the provisions of the Copyright Act 1956 (as amended). Any person or persons who do any unauthorised act in relation to this publication may be liable to criminal prosecution and civil claims for damages.

Author: William Potter
Illustrator: Rhys Jefferys
Design: Tokiko Morishima and Gina Wood
Editors: Donna Gregory and Becca Clunes
Design manager: Rosie Bellwood-Moyler
Editorial manager: Joe Harris

ISBN: 978-1-3988-4427-8
CH011596US
Supplier 29, Date 1024, PI 00008296

Printed in China

CONTENTS

Introducing astronomy	4
The history of astronomy	5
Messier objects and more	9

Chapter 1: The night sky

The night sky	10
Seasons	12
Planetary motion	14
Naming the stars	16
Constellations	17
Magnitude	18
The Milky Way	20

Chapter 2: Stargazing kit

Stargazing kit	22
Stargazing setup	24
Binoculars and telescopes	26
Mounts	28
Accessories	29
Keeping a log	30
Astrophotograpy	31
Star hopping	32
Planispheres and star maps	33
Top 10 sights	34

Chapter 3: Key constellations

Key constellations	36
Northern hemisphere	38
Southern hemisphere	39
Andromeda	40
Canis Major	42
Carina	43
Cassiopeia	44
Centaurus	45
Crux	46
Cygnus	47
Draco	48
Hercules	49
Hydra	50
Lyra	51
Orion	52
Sagittarius	54
Scorpius	55
Taurus	56
Ursa Major	58
Ursa Minor	59

Chapter 4: The solar system

Solar system	60
The Sun	62
The Moon	64
Lunar highlights	66
Mercury	68
Venus	69
Mars	70
Jupiter	72
Saturn	74
Uranus	76
Neptune	77
Dwarf planets	78
Kuiper belt and beyond	79
Comets	80
Asteroids	81
Meteors	82

Chapter 5: Deep sky

Deep sky	84
Life of a star	86
Multiple and variable stars	88
Galaxies	90
Nebulae	92
Taking it further	94

Glossary	96

INTRODUCING ASTRONOMY

On a clear night, as the Sun dips over the horizon, a universe of wonders slowly reveals itself. Stars and planets emerge, forming patterns in the sky. With the aid of binoculars or a small telescope, pinpricks of light are revealed as star clusters, patches of light as glowing nebulae or spiral galaxies, and shadows on the Moon as a rich landscape to explore.

The night sky always has something new to share, as constellations rise throughout the seasons and annual meteorite showers dazzle in the darkness. This book invites you to cast your eye on our Universe. We'll describe the kit you need, show you how to find your way across the sky, and point out highlights. The Moon is mapped in detail, the planets in the Solar System are explored, and the secrets of how stars are born, burn, and die are explained.

The Andromeda Galaxy

You'll never forget the first time you see Saturn's rings, the Andromeda Galaxy, or the Orion Nebula. All of these spectacles are easy to enjoy through the most basic of lenses. Once you're hooked, the night sky's the limit.

Saturn

The Orion Nebula

THE HISTORY OF ASTRONOMY

People have studied the heavens for thousands of years, recording the position of stars, the phases of the Moon, and the angle of the rising Sun in order to plan for sowing and harvesting, and to determine the dates for religious events.

STONE CALENDARS

In Europe, Asia, Africa, and the Americas, pyramids and stone circles were erected in Mesolithic times as celestial calendars, aligned with the movement of stars through the seasons, and marking the solstices and equinoxes.

NEBRA SKY DISK

Unearthed in Germany, this 3,600-year-old metal disk shows how the Sun, Moon, and stars fascinated Bronze-Age people. While it may look simplistic, details suggest some accurate observation of the skies took place. Gold bands on the rims mark the angle of the sunrise between solstices, while the group of golden stars may represent the Pleiades (page 57).

STAR GODDESS

Ancient Egyptian astronomers realized that annual floods from the River Nile followed the appearance of the bright star Sirius before sunrise in July. They represented the star as the goddess Sopdet.

ANCIENT RECORDS

Astronomers from ancient Babylon (in modern day Iraq) were among the first to record the names they had given to stars and track the movement of planets. Their studies, recorded on clay tablets around 700 BCE, were the foundation for much of what followed.

NEXT STEPS IN ASTRONOMY

Ancient Greek philosophers believed that the Earth was at the center of the Universe, with planets and stars following circular orbits around a stationary Earth. They used geometry to work out that the Earth, Moon, and planets were spherical and closely estimated Earth's circumference.

Islamic scholars

A NEW SPIN

In fifth-century India, the astronomer Aryabhata suggested that Earth itself was spinning, rather than the stars moving around Earth.

ISLAMIC INNOVATIONS

From the seventh to the fifteenth centuries, Islamic astronomy scholars' work led to improvements in observations—including the recording of a major supernova—and accurate measurements of time and celestial movement. The astrolabe, a device used to measure time and latitude using the position of the Moon and stars, became an essential aid for navigators.

Nicolaus Copernicus

SOLAR SYSTEM

In the sixteenth century, most European astronomers believed that the planets and Sun revolved around the Earth. Working before the invention of the telescope, the astronomer Nicolaus Copernicus published an alternative theory in 1543. Observations by other astronomers supported Copernicus's theory that the Earth and other planets orbit the Sun.

RENAISSANCE AND ENLIGHTENMENT

In 1610, Italian Galileo Galilei used the newly invented telescope to discover moons orbiting Jupiter and track the phases of Venus. His work backed the Copernican model, which put him in conflict with the Church's belief that Earth was at the center of the Universe. Galileo was put under house arrest for his final years.

How the planets remained in orbit was unexplained until the English scientist Isaac Newton presented his laws of gravity in 1687, proposing that the same force that caused objects to fall downward kept the planets in place.

Galileo Galilei

BLUE PLANET

The eighteenth century saw a boom in observatory building and sponsored study. William Herschel, a German musician turned astronomer, began crafting high-quality telescopes and observed several binary stars. In 1781 he discovered a new planet, Uranus.

A NEW SCIENCE

In 1846, the planet Neptune was discovered. Astronomers knew where to look as they had calculated its position from discrepencies in the orbit of Uranus.

The nineteenth century saw the birth of astrophysics, as scientists investigated the size, temperature, mass, and make-up of stars by studying different wavelengths of light.

THE EXPANDING UNIVERSE

It was not until the 1920s that galaxies beyond our Milky Way were confirmed when the US astronomer Edwin Hubble identified the Andromeda Galaxy (page 41, and below). The Universe was suddenly far larger than previously understood and still expanding.

The Andromeda Galaxy

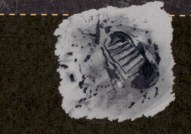

TO THE MOON AND BACK

The Space Race of the mid-twentieth century led to great leaps in technology, including the first artificial satellites, robotic space probes to the Moon, Venus, and Mars, the first human spaceflights, and ultimately the first humans on the Moon in 1969.

An observatory

ASTRONOMY TODAY

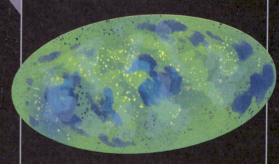

TO INFINITY, AND BEYOND

Astronomy has continued to advance with huge observatories on Earth and telescopes in space mapping the stars. These observatories can use visible light, as well as other frequencies in the electromagnetic spectrum, including radio waves, ultraviolet and infrared radiation, X-rays, and gamma rays.

Robotic probes have toured the Solar System and landed on planets, comets, and asteroids, collecting data. In recent years scientists have produced an image of a black hole at the center of a galaxy, detected thousands of planets outside our Solar System, and mapped the leftover radiation from the birth of the Universe (above).

MESSIER OBJECTS AND MORE

The Messier Catalog, compiled in the eighteenth century, provides a checklist for the keen collector of sightings of deep-sky objects.

M45: The Pleiades

M51: Whirlpool Galaxy

ANYTHING BUT COMETS

Eighteenth-century French astronomer Charles Messier was a keen observer of comets. He was distracted by other faint lights in the sky that could be mistaken for his beloved comets. To avoid confusion, he compiled a list of sights in the night sky that were NOT comets. The list became known as the Messier Catalog. Successfully finding all of the 110 items in the Messier Catalog is now an astronomy badge of honor, with some people trying to see them all in one night!

Charles Messier

NGC AND IC

The Messier Catalog has been superseded by lengthier lists that cover both hemispheres. The New General Catalogue (NGC) contains a phenomenal 8,000 deep-sky objects. The Index Catalogue (IC) adds a further 5,000. Of these 13,000 stellar objects, most are beyond the range of the amateur—they are far too distant and faint to see without professional equipment, but new stargazers need not worry about running out of targets.

BEGINNER-FRIENDLY CHECKLIST

The Messier Catalog includes a mix of clusters, nebulae, and galaxies up to M110, a distant galaxy neighboring Andromeda. Messier used a 10-cm (4-in) refracting telescope in his Paris observatory, so everything on the list can be seen with a small telescope in the northern hemisphere.

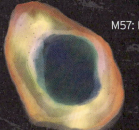

M57: Ring Nebula

CHAPTER 1: THE NIGHT SKY

The night sky can seem overwhelming at first, with countless stars and patterns, but once you become familiar with a few constellations, how they relate to each other, and how your view of the sky changes through the seasons, you'll soon learn to navigate the heavens.

THE CELESTIAL SPHERE

Imagine a sphere around Earth that includes all the stars we can see above us. This is the celestial sphere, a helpful way for us to locate objects in the night sky. The celestial sphere is divided into hemispheres to match Earth's northern and southern hemisphere. It also has poles and an equator.

On Earth, any point can be identified using the imaginary lines of longitude (running from pole to pole) and latitude (running parallel to the equator). The celestial sphere has equivalent lines so that a stellar object can be mapped. These measurements are called right ascension and declination.

Right ascension (RA) is the distance east or west of the celestial meridian. The celestial meridian is an imagined line that passes through the Earth's poles and the vernal equinox or First Point of Aries (page 36) where the Sun crosses between the northern and southern celestial hemispheres. Right ascension is measured in hours, minutes, and seconds. 24 hours is 360 degrees, 1 hour is 15 degrees.

Declination (DEC) is the position north or south of the celestial equator. It is measured in degrees (°) and arc minutes ('). (1 degree = 60 arc minutes.) For the northern celestial hemisphere, degrees go from 0° to 90° at the north pole. In the southern hemisphere, degrees go from 0° to -90° at the south pole.

Celestial equator

Vernal equinox

Right ascension

South celestial pole

North celestial pole

Celestial meridian

Declination

THE ECLIPTIC

The ecliptic is the apparent path taken by the Sun, as seen from Earth. The planets in the Solar System also stay close to this line as they follow an almost flat elliptical path around the Sun. Earth's axis is tilted by about 23.5°, so the ecliptic appears at this angle to the celestial equator.

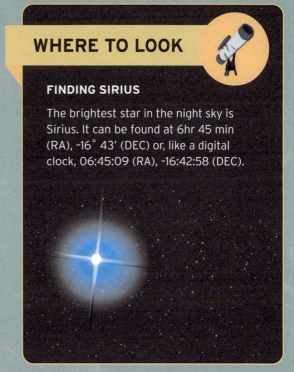

WHERE TO LOOK

FINDING SIRIUS

The brightest star in the night sky is Sirius. It can be found at 6hr 45 min (RA), -16° 43' (DEC) or, like a digital clock, 06:45:09 (RA), -16:42:58 (DEC).

SEASONS

As the Earth turns on its axis each day and orbits the Sun over a year, different groups of stars come into view through time.

Earth's orbit of 365.25 days around the Sun is slightly elliptical, putting it closer to the Sun at certain times of the year, but it is our planet's tilt that has more of an effect on our seasons. Earth spins around its axis, an imaginary line through its poles, completing one rotation each day. The 23.4° angle of Earth's axis means that the northern and southern hemispheres spend part of the year tilted toward or tilted away from the Sun. The northern hemisphere leans toward the Sun in June and experiences summer, while the southern hemisphere leans away and goes through winter. In December, the opposite occurs.

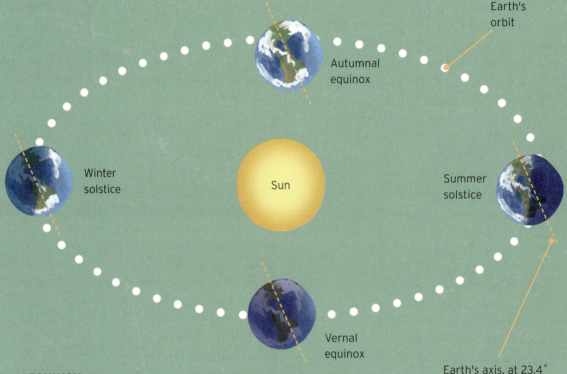

EQUINOX

Earth's tilt affects the length of the days. Through summer, the Sun stays above the horizon for longer, with the longest day occurring on the summer solstice around June 21. The shortest day, the winter solstice, occurs six months later. When the days and night are of equal length we have what is called an equinox.

DIRECT SUNLIGHT

The Sun's rays hit Earth at different angles. Where the Sun is lowest in the sky, in the farthest north and south, the angle is greatest and the rays are absorbed by a greater area of atmosphere, so these areas remain relatively cool. Between the tropics, the Sun's rays hit the Earth more directly, so these areas are warmer.

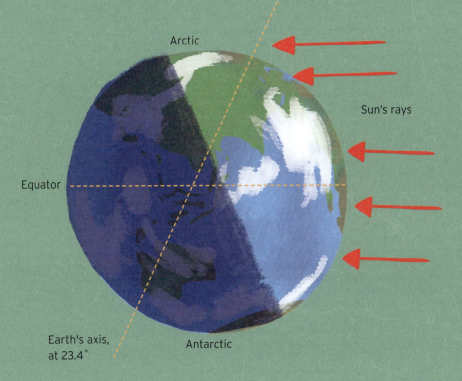

VIEWING TIME

For stargazers, summer means warmer and drier nights but few (or even no) hours of darkness in the evening. Winter means cold weather but longer and darker nights for viewing.

PLANETARY MOTION

While the stars can easily be found among the constellations in the night sky, tracking planets requires more detective work. Each planet in our Solar System is moving in its own orbital path, and their trajectories and the length of time their orbits take are all different. However, we can use the observations of past scientists to track them in our night sky.

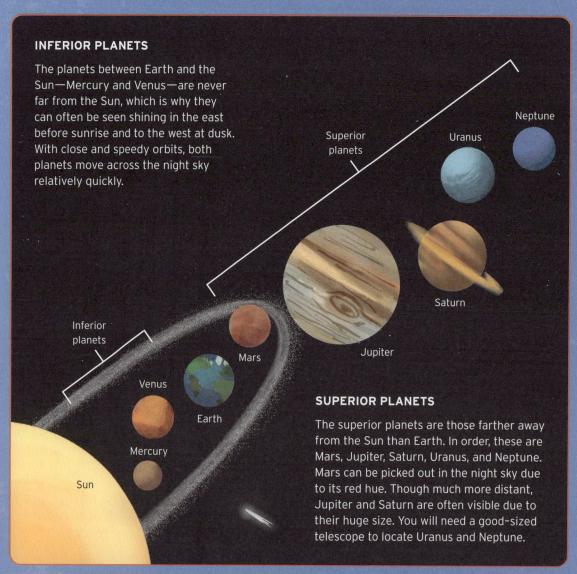

INFERIOR PLANETS

The planets between Earth and the Sun—Mercury and Venus—are never far from the Sun, which is why they can often be seen shining in the east before sunrise and to the west at dusk. With close and speedy orbits, both planets move across the night sky relatively quickly.

SUPERIOR PLANETS

The superior planets are those farther away from the Sun than Earth. In order, these are Mars, Jupiter, Saturn, Uranus, and Neptune. Mars can be picked out in the night sky due to its red hue. Though much more distant, Jupiter and Saturn are often visible due to their huge size. You will need a good-sized telescope to locate Uranus and Neptune.

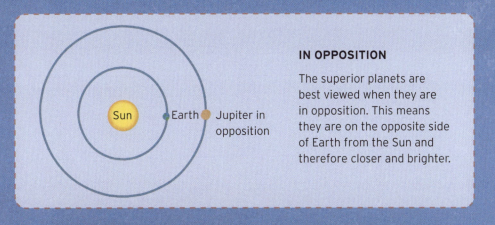

IN OPPOSITION

The superior planets are best viewed when they are in opposition. This means they are on the opposite side of Earth from the Sun and therefore closer and brighter.

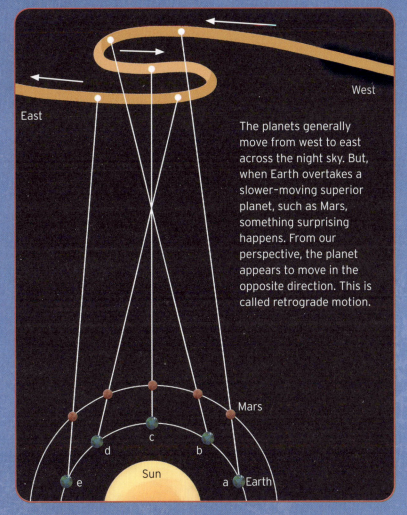

The planets generally move from west to east across the night sky. But, when Earth overtakes a slower-moving superior planet, such as Mars, something surprising happens. From our perspective, the planet appears to move in the opposite direction. This is called retrograde motion.

NAMING THE STARS

The brightest stars have traditional names given to them by the earliest astronomers but they also have an official designation based on their brightness and location within a constellation.

Most of the bright stars in the night sky retain the names given to them thousands of years ago by Babylonian, Greek, or Arabic astronomers. These include Ursa Major's Alcor (Arabic for "the forgotten one"), Arcturus (Greek for "guardian of the bear"), and Canis Minor's Sirius (Greek for "the scorcher").

In 1603, the German astronomer Johann Bayer set out to produce a more systematic naming system, using the 24 letters of the Greek alphabet to label stars within each constellation, from the brightest (alpha, α) to the second brightest (beta, β), and so on. When the 24 letters are used up, small Roman letters (a, b, c, etc.) are used.

Here is how the five brightest stars in the constellation of Cassiopeia (page 44) are named:

CASSIOPEIA

Some of the stars in the Cassiopeia constellation are also known by their Arabic names:
Alpha Cassiopeiae—Schdir
Beta Cassiopeiae—Caph
Delta Cassiopeiae—Ruchbah

Epsilon (ε) Cassiopeiae

Gamma (γ) Cassiopeiae

Beta (β) Cassiopeiae

Delta (δ) Cassiopeiae

Alpha (α) Cassiopeiae

CONSTELLATIONS

The night sky is divided into 88 officially recognized constellations, each with its own boundary. The list is based on those identified by the Ancient Greek astronomers Hipparchus and Ptolemy, with additions from the sixteenth and eighteenth centuries.

Different cultures invented their own pictures in the stars. Traditional Chinese star maps featured up to 283 constellations, with names reflecting scenes from court and daily life. Indian astronomers divided the sky along the ecliptic into 27 sections called Nakshatras with names such as "the bearer," "the deer's head," and "the root." The North American Navajo culture saw Orion (page 52) as a warrior named Átse Ats'oosí.

Today, astronomers use the naming system of the IAU (International Astronomical Union). The constellations include an area of sky as well as the stars that can be joined to make a picture. These bordered areas fit together like jigsaw pieces to cover the entire sky.

PTOLEMY

Around 140 CE, the Greek mathematician and astronomer Ptolemy compiled a list of over a thousand stars and 48 constellations (based on earlier work by Hipparchus) which he published in his book *Almagest*. His list became the basis for the catalog of 88 constellations that we use today.

The jigsaw of constellations

ASTERISMS

Asterisms are star patterns that are smaller than constellations. The Big Dipper (also known as the Plough) is probably the best known—it is in the constellation of Ursa Major.

MAGNITUDE

The brightness of a star in the sky not only depends on how much light it gives off but also its distance from Earth and anything blocking its path. Astronomers use a measurement called magnitude to compare differences.

A star's brightness as it appears to an astronomer on Earth is called its apparent magnitude. In 1856, the English astronomer Norman Pogson refined the classification system. In Pogson's system, each level of magnitude is 2.5 times brighter than the one below. So, a first-magnitude star is 100 times brighter than a sixth-magnitude star. The scale includes negative numbers. The smaller the number, and the more negative, the brighter the star appears, while the higher the number, the less bright the star seems.

The system applies not just to stars but to planets and moons. Our Sun has a magnitude of –26.7, while the Full Moon is –12.6 and Mars at its brightest is –3. The brightest star in the night sky is Sirius. This has a magnitude of –1.5.

On a clear night, with the unaided eye, you might be able to see stars with an apparent magnitude in the range of –1.5 (Sirius) to 5 or 6. To see stars of a greater magnitude, you will need binoculars or a telescope.

HIPPARCHUS

In the second century BCE, the Greek astronomer Hipparchus described the stars that he saw in the northern hemisphere. He used a classification system with six levels of brightness. This system was used for hundreds of years.

APPARENT MAGNITUDE

	Visual Limit	Magnitude
	Naked-eye	6
	Through binoculars	9.5
	Though 6-inch telescope	13
	Though 200-inch telescope	20
	Hubble Space Telescope	30

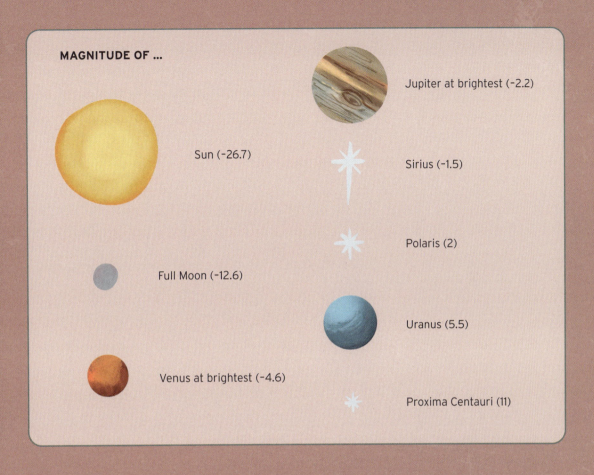

MAGNITUDE OF ...

Jupiter at brightest (-2.2)

Sun (-26.7)

Sirius (-1.5)

Polaris (2)

Full Moon (-12.6)

Uranus (5.5)

Venus at brightest (-4.6)

Proxima Centauri (11)

ABSOLUTE MAGNITUDE

How bright would the stars be if they were all the same distance away? Absolute magnitude is a measure of a star's brightness from 10 parsecs (32.6 light-years) away. On this scale, the Sun's absolute magnitude is 4.8, while Deneb, a blue-white supergiant star in the constellation of Cygnus (page 47) has an absolute magnitude of -7.5. Deneb is 19 times more massive than our Sun and is thought to be up to 196,000 times brighter.

Deneb

Sun

THE MILKY WAY

All the stars we see with the unaided eye belong to our home galaxy, which is known as the Milky Way.

On clear, dark nights, away from light pollution, you may be lucky enough to see an area of sky, thick with stars and dust clouds, arching overhead. This is our view toward the center of the Milky Way. This barred spiral galaxy is 100,000 light years in diameter and contains hundreds of billions of stars and possibly 100 billion planets. Our Solar System is located about 26,000 light years from its center, in the Orion arm. The entire galaxy is rotating and it will take our Sun about 250 million years to complete one orbit.

Seen face on, the Milky Way would resemble a cosmic pinwheel with a dense, brilliant center. There are thought to be four major and two minor spiral arms extending from this center but there are stars between these, too. The stars in the arms are younger and brighter so they appear more luminous. At the heart of the galaxy, hidden from view by dust and gas, is a supermassive black hole (page 54).

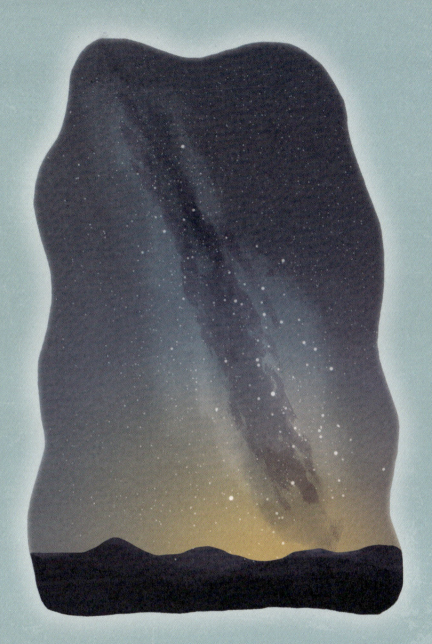

COSMIC SPLASH

You will need to be away from light pollution on a cloud-free night to see the Milky Way. Our galaxy gets its name from the Greek "galaktikòs kýklos," meaning "milky circle." In legend, it was caused by milk spilled across the heavens by the gods. Only 100 years ago the Milky Way was thought to contain all the stars of the Universe. We now know that our galaxy is one of trillions.

CHAPTER 2: STARGAZING KIT

The first astronomers didn't have binoculars or telescopes. They mapped the motion of the stars and planets with the naked eye and measuring instruments. You can see a lot without equipment, though a pair of binoculars can be really helpful.

Start outside your own home on a clear, dry night, ideally away from street lighting, and gaze upward. Give your eyes several minutes to get adjusted to the darkness—more and more stars should become visible. You may already know a few star patterns, such as the constellation Orion or the Big Dipper (Plough) asterism.

Get familiar with the constellations and how they relate to each other so that you can navigate from one to the next. You can use this book or pick up a star map or planisphere (page 33) as a guide. Some stars are much brighter than others. The Moon can be admired without lenses, as it goes through its phases. If you are in an area with little light pollution, you might even see the sweep of the Milky Way (page 21) across the sky.

Over the course of an evening some constellations will drop out of view, and new ones will rise as the Earth turns. Over the course of a year, the constellations on view will change. Once you're hooked, you'll want to take your stargazing to the next level and that's where binoculars and telescopes come in.

If you consult a star chart, or you want to make notes, use a red light or a lamp with a red filter. This will keep your eyes adapted to the darkness.

NATURE'S FIREWORKS

Several times throughout the year, the night sky rewards stargazers with a spectacular display of "shooting stars." There are meteor showers (page 83) almost every month, with January's Quadrantids, August's Perseids, and December's Geminids particularly impressive. While you can know the region of sky they spring from, meteors are unpredictable and too fast to track with a telescope. Just get comfortable and enjoy the show with your naked eyes. A long-exposure photograph (see page 31) may capture several meteors at once.

STARGAZING SETUP

Where and when to watch the stars? And what to wear? You need to be prepared to spend some quality time outside to be an astronomer. Wrap up for cold nights and have a plan.

Stargazing means spending a lot of time outdoors after dark. In summer, it's warm but the nights are short. You have to stay up later and the sky can remain light until it's very late. In the far north, it might not get dark enough to see stars at all! In winter, you'll have a lot more time for stargazing but it can be cold and cloudy. Either way, you'll need to plan ahead.

WHERE TO VIEW

A backyard, garden, or rooftop is ideal as a place to start stargazing. You don't have to carry any equipment far and there's shelter nearby if you need it. Look for a spot where street lighting or lights from nearby houses doesn't reach but where you have as wide a view of the sky as possible. Planets spend a lot of time just above the horizon, so an open space is good.

LIGHT POLLUTION

Urban environments mean a lot of street lighting, making it hard to get a sharp, contrasting view of the night sky. Even if you live in the countryside you may still see a glow on the horizon from a nearby town. If you can't get away from it, find a stargazing spot in the shadows where your eyes can stay adjusted to the dark.

WHAT TO WEAR

Wear layers. A warm hat and coat are recommended, as are fingerless gloves, so you can turn the pages of guides, adjust the focus on your telescope, or check a stargazing app. If you're away from shelter, you may want to wear a waterproof jacket too, in case of a surprise shower.

SITTING PRETTY

You'll be spending a lot of time being still, looking through a viewfinder. Have a stool or fold-up chair with you. If you plan to stay out long, pack a few snacks and something to drink. (A hot drink in a vacuum flask is very welcome on a cold night.)

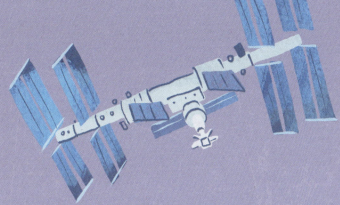

ALWAYS tell an adult when you plan to be outdoors after dark, even if you are just stargazing at home.

IN ORBIT

In recent years the number of artificial satellites in orbit has increased immensely. You will certainly see many lights crossing the skies at speed. One light you might want to track, though, is the International Space Station (ISS). This orbits Earth 16 times a day. You can find out when it is next due over your area at spotthestation.nasa.gov

BINOCULARS AND TELESCOPES

To see detail and fainter, more distant objects in the night sky, you're going to need some help. For new stargazers who want to travel light, binoculars are a great choice. For deep space and planet watching, telescopes are the way to go.

BINOCULARS

Binoculars are a good first choice for stargazing. They are inexpensive and portable, so you can easily take them to look at the stars in places with little light pollution, even on vacation.

Binoculars allow a wide field of view (area of visible sky), so you can take in the whole of the Andromeda Galaxy (page 41), for example. When choosing binoculars you need to look at two numbers. The first is the magnification, the second the aperture or diameter of the objective lenses. So 10 x 50 means 10 times magnification of a view through a 50 mm (2 in)-wide lens.

The larger the objective lens, the more light you can collect from faint objects. For astronomy, look for binoculars with an aperture 5 times the number of the magnification.

For a young stargazer, 8 x 40 is a good size, while adults may prefer the larger and heavier 10 x 50 size. Try different models in store to see what you are most comfortable with.

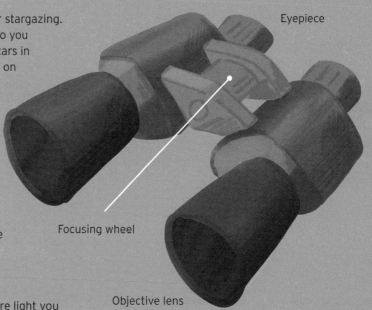

Eyepiece

Focusing wheel

Objective lens

FLIPPED VIEW

Due to the arrangement of lenses and mirrors, what you see through the eyepiece in astronomical telescopes is both upside down and flipped left to right, something you will get used to.

TELESCOPES

To see farther into deep space you need a telescope. There is a huge range of different kinds of telescopes available over a wide price range.

REFRACTING TELESCOPE

Refracting telescopes have a curved objective lens at the front which bends light to a focusing lens and to an eyepiece. Most entry-level telescopes are refractors. They are light, easy to set up and provide good views of the Moon and planets.

REFLECTING TELESCOPE

Reflecting telescopes use curved mirrors to collect light and focus it toward the eyepiece. Generally, reflectors will give you larger apertures and better views of deep-space objects for the same price as a smaller refracting telescope. Telescopes with an aperture around 100-130 mm (4-5 in) are good enough for viewing the planets of the Solar System. For deep-space objects such as nebulae, you'll need something in the 150-200 mm (6-8 in) range, but that means a model that is heavy and harder to move.

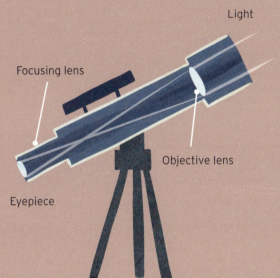

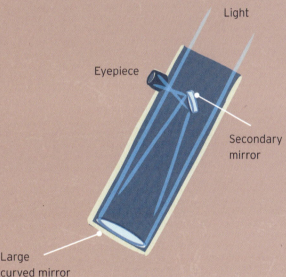

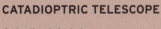

CATADIOPTRIC TELESCOPE

Catadioptric telescopes are reflecting telescopes that use a corrective lens to focus within a shorter tube.

Many models are fitted with a computer-controlled motorized mount (page 28).

DOBSONIAN TELESCOPE

Dobsonians are large reflecting telescopes set on a box-like mount with a swiveling base. Their simple design makes them an affordable choice for stargazers wanting a telescope with a large aperture.

MOUNTS

You will need a mount to hold your telescope. The two most common designs are the altazimuth and equatorial, on an adjustable tripod. The mount you choose will also depend on its weight—light and portable or heavy but sturdy.

ALTAZIMUTH

The altazimuth or altaz mount moves along two axes from the horizon:

Altitude—up and down

Azimuth—side to side

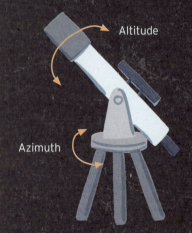

Altitude

Azimuth

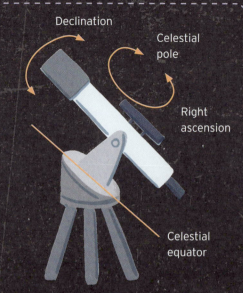

Declination

Celestial pole

Right ascension

Celestial equator

EQUATORIAL

Equatorial mounts need to be lined up with the celestial equator (page 10) and pole. They then move in the two directions used for mapping stars:

Declination—up and down

Right ascension—side to side

By being aligned with the celestial equator, these mounts can easily track the rotation of stars in the sky. Many equatorial mounts are motor-driven, ideal for long-exposure astrophotography (page 31).

COMPUTER CONTROL

A set-up known as GoTo can be fitted to equatorial or fork mounts to locate objects across the night sky. With GoTo, you tap the coordinates or catalog numbers of what you want to see into a handset and the motorized drive will line up the telescope for you. GoTo removes the effort of looking for specific sights but the set-up can be pricey.

ACCESSORIES

The options for adding to your astronomy kit are seemingly endless. A quality eyepiece is essential, while filters and apps can enhance your experience of stargazing.

EYEPIECES

Most telescopes come with an eyepiece. At some point you may want to invest in more or better-quality models. You can switch between eyepieces to change the magnification of your view.

Eyepieces are sold according to their focal length. The lower the focal length the higher the magnification. A 25 mm (1.25 in) eyepiece is the most useful to begin with.

Rather than investing in a whole new eyepiece, you can choose a Barlow lens that fits between your eyepiece and telescope, magnifying 2 or 3 times what you would see. But, while high magnification might sound appealing, it means you will only see a small area of sky through your eyepiece. This makes it hard to locate an object and keep it in view.

FILTERS

Filters can be fitted between your telescope and the eyepiece. One of the most useful is a light pollution reduction (LPR) filter, which helps reduce the glare from street lighting.

A neutral density filter also reduces glare, providing better contrast for viewing bright objects such as the Moon.

An ultra high contrast (UHC) filter makes the background darker so deep-space objects, such as nebulae, stand out more.

Colored filters can help you see more detail on planets.

KEEPING A LOG

Building a record of your stargazing experiences is a good habit to keep. You never know when you might spot something significant.

Choose a good-quality, sturdy book for your notes. You'll want to keep it for years. Your logbook will provide a diary of your stargazing discoveries and be a useful tool for future evenings under the stars. A meticulous record of viewings may also provide a service for other astronomers. Amateur astronomers have been known to discover comets.

RECORD KEEPING

Good notes are invaluable. Even records of failure will help you seek out better maps or the right equipment to locate that elusive goal.

Things to record in your astronomy journal include:

DATE, TIME, PLACE, CONDITIONS

- At what hour was it dark enough to view?
- How clear was the sky? Did cloud or glare from light pollution or the Moon spoil your viewing?

KIT

This is useful information if you want to recreate a sighting.

- What telescope did you use? Did you use any filters?
- Which eyepiece and magnification did you use?

TARGETS

It's a good idea to have a plan before you head out to stargaze.

- What were you hoping to see?
- Did you succeed in viewing all of your targets?

SKETCHES

Draw sketches of any sightings that interested you.

- Were there stripes on Jupiter? Was Venus in phase? Perhaps there was a star pattern that led you to a hard-to-find nebula.

ASTROPHOTOGRAPHY

Keeping a visual record of your stargazing highlights can be very satisfying, as well as useful. With a phone or digital camera you can capture colorful nebula and stunning star trails.

WORKING WITH A TELESCOPE

You can take a photo through your telescope with a regular camera or phone by using an attachment that locks it to the eyepiece. But to photograph planets and deep-space objects you will need a telescope on a motorized mount (page 28) so the object remains in view during the long exposure.

CAMERA ONLY

Taking photos of the night sky requires a long exposure to pick out the dim light. You will need to use a tripod to keep your camera steady and, ideally, a remote shutter release. A wide angle lens works best for framing the sky and some landscape.

You can get decent pictures with just a phone. You will need to keep it very still, so use a tripod attachment. Set it to night mode with a long exposure—ideally at least 30 seconds.

STAR TRAILS

To capture the motion of the stars around the celestial pole (page 10), first locate the pole star (page 32, 46) then find a good framing for your photo, with little light pollution and some interesting landscape.

Set your camera for very long exposure. Digital cameras can overheat if left running for long periods so try taking 10 to 20 pictures, each with 3-minute exposures. You can blend them together later, using a computer.

STAR HOPPING

There are a bewildering number of stars in the sky. It takes time to figure out what's what, but once you get to know one or two asterisms, star hopping will lead you to the next.

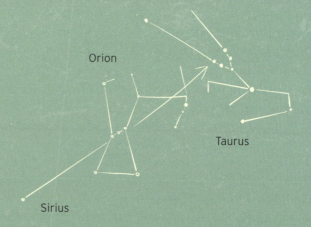

Orion

Taurus

Sirius

STARTING POINTS

There are several constellations and asterisms (star patterns smaller than constellations) that almost leap out of the night sky. Easy to recognize and easy to find, these are the best starting points for your tour of the night sky.

ORION

The three stars in the belt of Orion the Hunter (page 52) appear in a straight line. From these, you can find the rest of the constellation. Follow a line from the belt toward a bright star and you will find the V-shaped head of Taurus the bull (page 56). In the opposite direction, you can follow the line to Sirius (page 42), the brightest star in the sky.

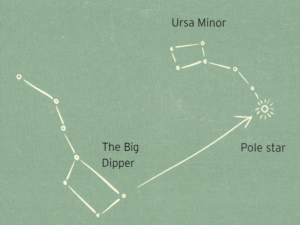

Ursa Minor

The Big Dipper

Pole star

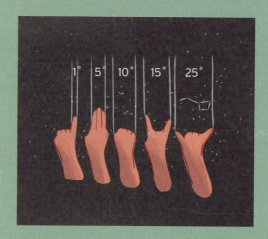

THE BIG DIPPER (PLOUGH)

In the northern hemisphere, the Big Dipper or Plough is a saucepan-like pattern of stars in the large constellation Ursa Major (page 58).

Two stars that form the Big Dipper provide a useful pointer to the northern pole star. Follow a line from the stars, as above, to the next bright star. This is Polaris, the tip of the tail on Ursa Minor (page 59).

DISTANCES

To estimate distances across the celestial hemisphere (page 10) you can use your fingers to measure degrees. Hold up a hand at arm's length and raise a finger to mark 1° or the span of your hand to mark 25°. (If you have small hands, the number of degrees will be fewer.)

PLANISPHERES AND STAR MAPS

Just as there are maps for drivers to navigate routes on land, there are maps of the skies above to lead astronomers to major sights.

PLANISPHERE

A planisphere is made of two sheets of card or plastic, one showing a map of the constellations, with the ecliptic and bright deep-sky objects in the night sky, and the other providing a rotating window of the map. Turn the top sheet around to match the date and hour you are stargazing and it will reveal which constellations are on view. Align the planisphere with north and you can now use it as a guide.

STAR MAP

For a more detailed view, a star atlas maps the sky in sections and includes stars visible down to magnitude 6.5. Stars are shown in different sizes depending on their magnitude (page 18). Objects marked on the maps include nebulae, binary stars, clusters, and galaxies.

APPS

Apps can be very useful to help you get familiar with the night sky and its many constellations, and especially for locating planets. These apps use your tablet or phone's inbuilt GPS to work out your location and viewing direction. Using satellite information, they project the position of stellar objects on to your phone screen so you can hold it up to the stars and see the names of what is above you. Most include a helpful night-vision mode. There are many apps to choose from, some free (with paid-for extras). Check online for the best recommended.

TOP 10 SIGHTS

You have your kit and a clear starry night. You're ready to go but, with so much choice, what do you look for? Here's a hit-list of 10 stellar sights to seek out.

1. THE MOON

You might think you've seen enough of the Moon, but through binoculars or a telescope you can get up close and explore every sea, mountain, and crater. Choose a night when the Moon is in phase so the shadows are deeper, bringing out more detail. (See page 64.)

2. SATURN'S RINGS

When this gas giant is above the horizon, it's a must see. A medium telescope reveals the famous rings, and you may also spy a number of its moons nearby. (See page 74.)

3. JUPITER AND MOONS

Through a telescope you may be able to pick out stripes or even the red spot on Jupiter, signs of constant storm clouds swirling around the Solar System's largest planet. The four large Galilean moons form a line on either side. (See page 72.)

4. ALBIREO

Through a telescope, Albireo, the fifth brightest star in the cross-shaped constellation of Cygnus, is revealed as a double—one large and orange, the other smaller and bright blue. (See page 47.)

5. HERCULES GLOBULAR CLUSTER

Binoculars will separate a blurry mass into a a spectacular, sparkling cluster of stars. (See page 49.)

6. ANDROMEDA GALAXY

If it was bright enough, we would see our nearest neighboring galaxy as three widths of the Moon wide. Through binoculars you'll be able to make out its bright center and the faint shape of its spiraling arms, plus two more distant galaxies, M32 and M110. (See page 40.)

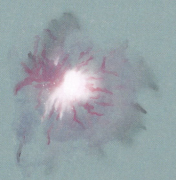

7. ORION NEBULA

The largest and brightest nebula in the sky is also the easiest to find, beside Orion's sword. This sprawling fan of gas and dust is a nursery for new stars. (See page 52.) Southern hemisphere viewers should seek out the equally impressive Carina Nebula. (See page 43.)

8. CRAB NEBULA

When you find the Crab Nebula, you're looking at history. Seen as a supernova by Chinese astronomers in 1054, it is now a mass of illuminated gas and the first stellar object listed in the Messier catalog. (See page 56.)

9. COALSACK NEBULA

A nebula with a difference. Rather than a glowing fan of gas, the Coalsack Nebula near Crux in the southern hemisphere is a massive patch of dust, visible through binoculars, obscuring the stars behind. (See page 46.)

10. PERSEIDS

You won't need a lens to appreciate this annual show. Shooting from the constellation Perseus in the month of August, this is the year's biggest and busiest meteor shower. (See page 82.)

CHAPTER 3: KEY CONSTELLATIONS

While the stories behind the figures, animals, and objects that form the constellations are mythological, these patterns of stars provide a useful map across the night sky. In this chapter, we look at the most interesting of the official constellations from both hemispheres, and the deep-sky objects worth seeking out through binoculars and telescopes. Where the constellations appear in the night sky above the horizon depends on the season and, indeed, which part of the world you view them from.

THE ZODIAC

The Sun and planets of the Solar System follow a path through the sky called the ecliptic (page 11), within a wider band called the zodiac. Over the course of one year the Sun crosses 13 constellations within the zodiac, 12 of which are associated with astrology. A thirteenth constellation, Ophiuchus, fills in a gap between Scorpio and Sagittarius.

The dates that the Sun passes through each zodiacal constellation (also the one most visible through the night) do not match the dates associated with their astrological signs. This is because of a gradual shift in the Earth's position over time and the different sizes of the constellations.

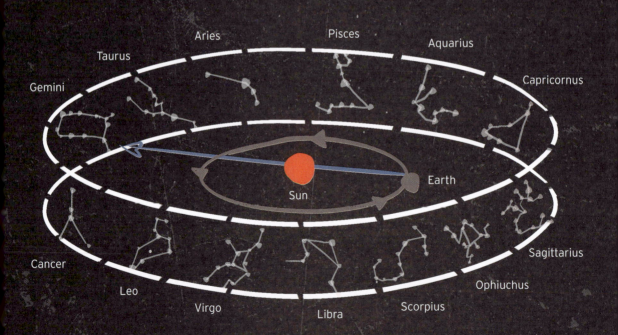

36

STORY OF THE STARS

The division of the ecliptic into 12 signs began with Babylonian astronomy 2,500 years ago. These divisions were adopted by astrologers, who believe that the stars and planets influence human events. There is no scientific evidence for this, but astrology remains popular and influential in some cultures.

AQUARIUS

The water-carrier constellation contains the Helix Nebula (NGC 7293), the closest planetary nebula to our Sun. This is visible through binoculars and small telescopes.

LEO

To find Leo look for the reverse question mark (the Sickle) forming the lion's head. Several spiral galaxies can be found beneath the lion's body using a small telescope.

GEMINI

Just away from Orion's raised arm (page 52), Gemini is an easy constellation to spot thanks to the two bright stars, Castor and Pollux, which represent the twins' heads. In mid-December each year, the meteor shower, the Geminids, radiates from close to Castor.

PISCES

To find Pisces, look for the ring of stars called the Circlet, that forms one of the pair of fish. Pisces contains the First Point of Aries or vernal (spring) equinox, the point where the Sun crosses the celestial equator from south to north (page 10). The coordinates of objects in the sky are measured from this point.

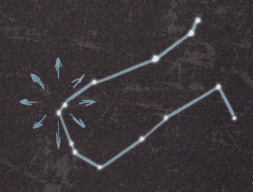

NORTHERN HEMISPHERE

Northern constellations appear to revolve around the pole star Polaris in Ursa Minor (page 59). Key constellations you can use to guide your way across the northern night skies include Ursa Major and its asterism the Big Dipper or the Plough (page 58), the cross of Cygnus (page 47), the W-shaped Cassiopeia (page 44), and, in winter, Orion with its prominent belt of three stars (page 52).

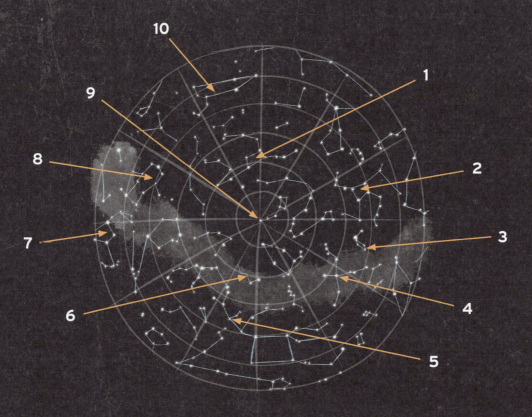

KEY TO NORTHERN HEMISPHERE:

1	Ursa Major	6	Cassiopeia
2	Hercules	7	Orion
3	Lyra	8	Gemini
4	Cygnus	9	Polaris
5	Andromeda	10	Leo

SOUTHERN HEMISPHERE

Key to finding your way around the southern night sky is locating Crux, the Southern Cross (page 46). The two stars forming the "upright" of this constellation point roughly to the south pole. From here, you can jump across to the two brightest stars of Centaurus (page 45), including the nearest naked-eye star to our Sun, Alpha Centauri. During summer, the belt of Orion (page 52) is a clear reference point, while the curve of Scorpius' tail (page 55) and the "teapot" of Sagittarius (page 54) are good springboards across the winter sky.

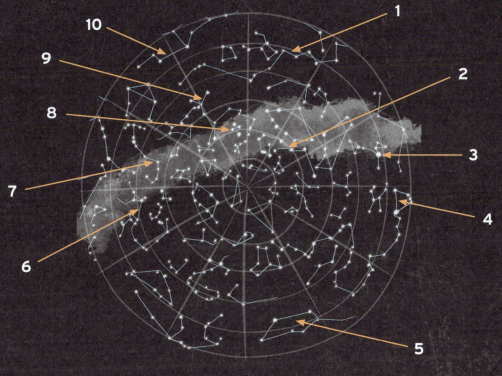

KEY TO SOUTHERN HEMISPHERE:

1	Hydra	6	Sagittarius
2	Carina	7	Scorpius
3	Canis Major	8	Crux
4	Orion	9	Centaurus
5	Cetus	10	Virgo

ANDROMEDA

The constellation of Andromeda contains the most distant object that can be seen with the naked eye—the Andromeda Galaxy. In 1764, astronomer Charles Messier (page 9) described it as a "spiral nebula." It wasn't until the 1920s that it was understood as another galaxy like our own.

1 ALMACH

Through a small telescope, Almach (also called Gamma Andromedae) is revealed as a pair—an orange giant with a fainter blue star.

2 TRIANGULUM

Close to the Andromeda constellation are three stars forming a triangle. This constellation was first recorded by the ancient Greeks. The Triangulum galaxy (M33) should be visible to its right.

3 ANDROMEDA GALAXY (M31)

On a clear night, the farthest object that can been seen with the naked eye is the Andromeda Galaxy—the nearest galaxy to our own. This spiral galaxy is 2.5 million light years away and, at approximately 200,000 light years in diameter, twice the width of the Milky Way. The Andromeda Galaxy is moving toward us and due to collide with the Milky Way in four to five billion years' time. Through binoculars, the galaxy appears as a fuzzy disk. If it was bright enough, it would cover an area of sky equivalent to the width of six Moons.

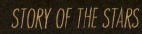

STORY OF THE STARS

In Greek mythology, Andromeda was the daughter of Cassiopeia (page 44), a princess chained to a rock as a sacrifice to a sea monster. She was rescued by the hero Perseus.

M32

M110

Through large telescopes, two more distant, elliptical galaxies, M32 and M110, can be seen, above and below the Andromeda Galaxy.

4 BLUE SNOWBALL NEBULA (NCC 7662)

This planetary nebula appears as a blue-green disk through a small telescope.

BEST VIEWED
Northern Hemisphere: August–February
Southern Hemisphere: October–December

CANIS MAJOR

Canis Major (the Greater Dog) contains the brightest star in the night sky. Sirius, also known as the Dog Star, is not only highly luminous but is relatively close to Earth, at 8.6 light years away.

1 SIRIUS
Twice the size of our Sun, Sirius is actually made up of two stars in a binary system with the white dwarf star Sirius B orbiting the brighter Sirius A every 50 years.

2 M41
On a clear night you might see M41 as a fuzzy patch on the chest of the Greater Dog. Through binoculars it is revealed as an open cluster of stars filling as much night sky as the full Moon.

STORY OF THE STARS
Canis Major is the larger of two dogs belonging to Orion the Hunter (page 52). In legend, the dog, named Laelaps, was so fast that no prey could escape it.

BEST VIEWED
Northern Hemisphere: December–March
Southern Hemisphere: November–April

CARINA

Carina is a constellation seen in the southern hemisphere. It features Canopus, a white supergiant, the second-brightest star in the southern sky, along with a spectacular nebula.

Canopus

STORY OF THE STARS

Carina is the keel or base of the legendary ship Argo, in which the Greek hero Jason and his crew of Argonauts set sail on a quest to find the Golden Fleece.

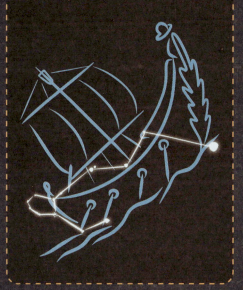

1 CARINA NEBULA (NGC 3372)

Larger and brighter than the Orion Nebula (page 50), the Carina Nebula, is home to Eta Carinae, a binary star reaching the end of its life and expected to go supernova.

2 SOUTHERN PLEIADES (IC 2602)

IC 2602 is a large cluster of stars that can be seen with the naked eye.

 BEST VIEWED
Southern Hemisphere: January–April

43

CASSIOPEIA

Visible all year round in the northern hemisphere, Cassiopeia is easily recognized as a large "W" in the night sky. The constellation features several open clusters and a double star.

STORY OF THE STARS

Ethiopian Queen Cassiopeia was the wife of King Cepheus. When she claimed to be more beautiful than the sea nymphs the Nereids, the enraged sea god Poseidon sent a monster to attack the coast of her kingdom.

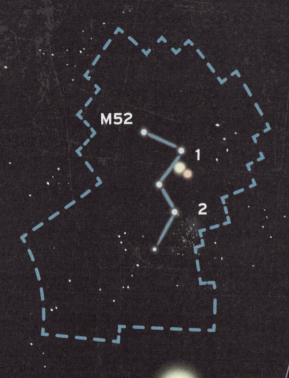

1 ETA CASSIOPEIAE

Eta Cassiopeiae is a double star featuring a yellow and red pairing that can be seen through a telescope. The fainter red star orbits the yellow star every 480 years.

2 MESSIER 103

Cassiopeia is positioned within the Milky Way, the area of the night sky with the densest area of stars. The pretty star clusters M103 (pictured here) and M52 are worth seeking out with binoculars.

BEST VIEWED
Northern Hemisphere: October–December

CENTAURUS

Southern Hemisphere constellation Centaurus, the Centaur, contains the closest star to our Sun and the brightest globular cluster seen from Earth.

1 OMEGA CENTAURI (NGC 5139)

Centaurus contains the largest and brightest globular cluster in the Milky Way, 17,090 light years from Earth. To the naked eye it appears as a blurry star. Binoculars reveal a dense ball with millions of stars. It may be the remains of a dwarf galaxy.

2 PROXIMA CENTAURI

Through a telescope, Rigil Kentaurus (Alpha Centauri) appears to be a binary star. But it's really a triple star system with faint Proxima Centauri nearby. At 4.2 light years away, this red dwarf is the closest star to our Sun.

STORY OF THE STARS

Centaurs were half-man-half-horse beings from Greek legend. Centaurus represents Chiron, a wise centaur who taught the heroes Jason and Hercules from his cave on Mount Pelion.

BEST VIEWED
Northern Hemisphere: May
Southern Hemisphere: April-June

CRUX

Crux, the Southern Cross, is a simple but distinctive constellation in the southern sky, found between the legs of Centaurus (page 45). It can be used as a guide to finding the south celestial pole.

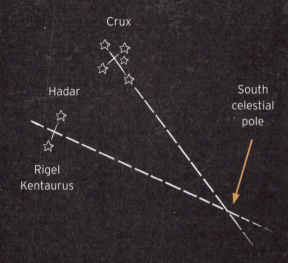

FINDING THE POLE

To locate the south celestial pole (and the direction south) draw a line down from Crux's longer axis. Draw a similar line between Centaurus' bright stars Rigel Kentaurus and Hadar. Where these two lines cross is the pole.

1 JEWEL BOX CLUSTER (NGC 4755)

Found beside the left-hand star on Crux's shorter axis is the Jewel Box Cluster, an open collection of 100 sparkling gems featuring a red supergiant surrounded by blue-white giants.

2 COALSACK NEBULA

Close to the Jewel Box is an inky patch of space named the Coalsack. This is a dark nebula with gas and dust blocking our view of the stars behind it.

BEST VIEWED
Southern Hemisphere: April-May

CYGNUS

Cygnus the swan appears as a large cross in the night sky. The swan's tail is the white supergiant Deneb, a star 200 times wider than our Sun. Cygnus X-1, halfway along the neck, is the site of the first confirmed black hole in our galaxy, though it is not possible to view through a telescope.

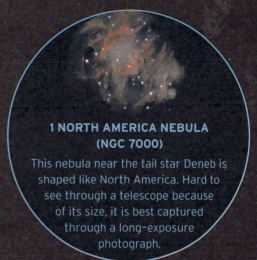

1 NORTH AMERICA NEBULA (NGC 7000)
This nebula near the tail star Deneb is shaped like North America. Hard to see through a telescope because of its size, it is best captured through a long-exposure photograph.

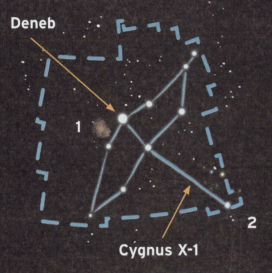

Deneb

Cygnus X-1

2 ALBIREO
Albireo is a stunning binary star marking the head and beak of the swan. Through a telescope you should be able to compare both its stars, one blue, the other bright orange.

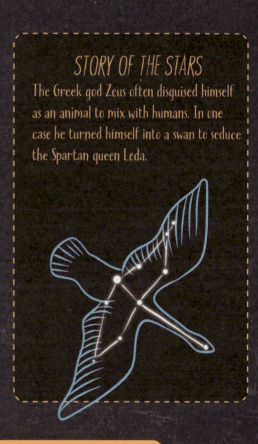

STORY OF THE STARS
The Greek god Zeus often disguised himself as an animal to mix with humans. In one case he turned himself into a swan to seduce the Spartan queen Leda.

BEST VIEWED
Northern Hemisphere: August–September
Southern Hemisphere: February–March

DRACO

Huge, winding Draco circles Ursa Minor (page 59). This huge constellation includes several double stars along its length and the dazzling but distant Cat's Eye Nebula.

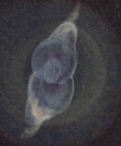

1 CAT'S EYE NEBULA (NGC 6543)

A small telescope should pick out the Cat's Eye Nebula as a small blue-green disk. Through a large telescope the nebula appears as a series of gas and dust shells bursting from a central star, leaving a trace that looks like a gigantic eye.

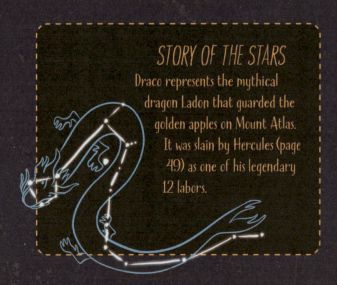

STORY OF THE STARS

Draco represents the mythical dragon Ladon that guarded the golden apples on Mount Atlas. It was slain by Hercules (page 49) as one of his legendary 12 labors.

2 NU DRACONIS

This double star on the dragon's head is easy to separate through binoculars or a small telescope. It is one of several double stars in the constellation.

BEST VIEWED
Northern Hemisphere: April–August

HERCULES

Heroic Hercules reaches out from a central keystone shape. On one side of this shape sits the northern sky's most spectacular globular cluster.

STORY OF THE STARS

Hercules was the super-strong half-human son of the Greek god Zeus (Jupiter) whose many adventures including a series of 12 labors. He is usually depicted wearing a lion skin, carrying a club and the golden apples he stole from the dragon Ladon (page 48).

1 HERCULES CLUSTER (M13)

Hercules' globular cluster is a must-see through a telescope. 25,000 light years from Earth and 145 light years across, the cluster boasts over 100,000 stars packed together.

BEST VIEWED
Northern Hemisphere: June–July
Southern Hemisphere: July–August

HYDRA

The largest of all the constellations, Hydra is a giant serpent of legend. Stretching a quarter of the way across the night sky, it take six hours to rise above the horizon but is hard to locate due to its low-magnitude stars.

1 GHOST OF JUPITER (NGC 3242)

The so-called "Ghost of Jupiter" is a planetary nebula that got its nickname because it resembles the planet Jupiter in size and pattern through a small telescope.

2 SOUTHERN PINWHEEL GALAXY (M83)

15 million light years away and similar in formation to our own Milky Way, the Southern Pinwheel Galaxy has spiral arms spinning from a bright central bar.

STORY OF THE STARS

The Hydra was a deadly serpent that Hercules (page 49) was sent to kill. In legend it had nine heads that grew back double for every one cut away.

BEST VIEWED
Northern Hemisphere: April–May
Southern Hemisphere: January–May

LYRA

Lyra, the Lyre, is a small and ancient constellation but it boasts the bright star Vega and the marvellous Ring Nebula.

2 DOUBLE DOUBLE

Near Vega is the fifth-brightest star seen from Earth, Epsilon Lyrae. Though a telescope this star is revealed as not just one but two double stars located about 160 light years away.

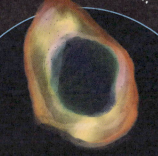

1 RING NEBULA (M57)

2,000 light years from Earth, this beautiful circular ring of hot gas released from a star, can be seen through a large telescope.

STORY OF THE STARS

A lyre is a small, hand-held harp. In Greek legend, when his wife, Eurydice, was killed by a snake bite, the musician Orpheus tried to bring her back by charming Hades, the god of the Underworld, with songs played on his lyre.

BEST VIEWED
Northern Hemisphere: June–October
Southern Hemisphere: July–September

Orion

Easily located thanks to the straight line of three stars that forms his belt, Orion the Hunter is home to the northern sky's most stunning nebula, and a red supergiant that is due to go supernova.

Betelgeuse

1 ORION NEBULA (M42)
Found below Orion's belt, the Orion Nebula is a must-see with the aid of binoculars or a telescope. About 24 light years across, the nebula is a nursery for new stars, within vast clouds of hydrogen gas and dust. Close by is M43, De Mairan's Nebula.

FOUR STARS
Once you find the Orion Nebula, look closely at the center. At the heart of the nebula you may see a group of four recently formed stars forming a shape called the Trapezium.

BEST VIEWED
Northern Hemisphere: October–February
Southern Hemisphere: November–March

Betelgeuse

BETELGEUSE

On Orion's shoulder is Betelgeuse, a red supergiant more than 500 times the size of our Sun. If placed in the position of our Sun, it would swallow everything up to about Jupiter. The star has greatly changed in brightness over the years and is likely to explode as a supernova within the next million years.

Orbit of Mercury

Orbit of Venus

Orbit of Earth

Orbit of Saturn   Orbit of Jupiter   Orbit of Mars

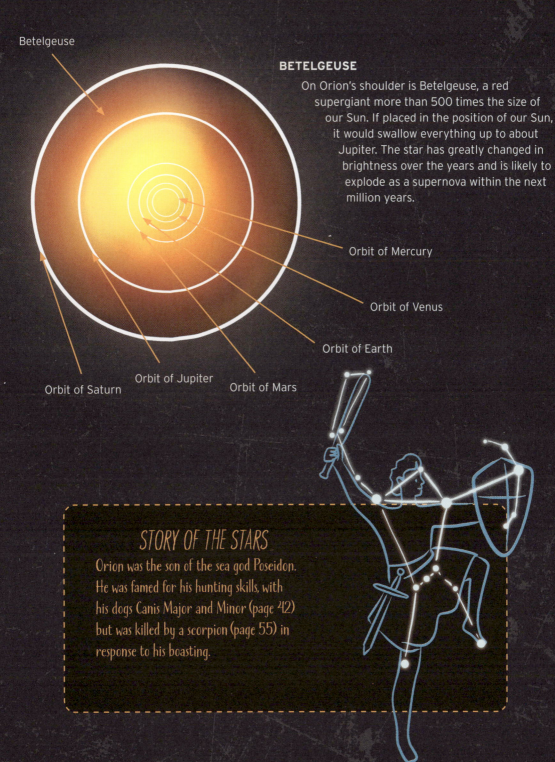

STORY OF THE STARS

Orion was the son of the sea god Poseidon. He was famed for his hunting skills, with his dogs Canis Major and Minor (page 42) but was killed by a scorpion (page 55) in response to his boasting.

SAGITTARIUS

Sagittarius is a zodiac sign which contains more Messier objects than any other constellations, as well as the black hole at the heart of the Milky Way. The constellation is most easily found by looking for the Teapot asterism.

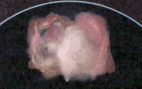

1 LAGOON NEBULA (M8)

Visible through binoculars as a gas cloud three times the width of the Moon, the Lagoon Nebula is lit by a cluster of young stars labelled NGC 6530. Through a telescope the nebula appears gray but long-exposure photos bring out its pretty pink hue.

2 SAGITTARIUS A*

Sagittarius A* is the location of a major source of radio waves which astronomers thought to be coming from a supermassive black hole at the center of our galaxy. An image of the accretion disk (the flattened ring of material around a black hole) was taken by a global network of radio telescopes in 2022.

STORY OF THE STARS

Sagittarius represents the zodiac sign of a half human–half horse centaur with a bow and arrow but the constellation has also been associated with the Babylonian god Nergal and the Greek satyr Crotus, the mythical inventor of archery.

BEST VIEWED
Northern Hemisphere: July–August
Southern Hemisphere: June–October

SCORPIUS

To find Scorpius, the scorpion, look for the distinctive hook at the end of its tail. Within the curve of the tail is an area packed with star clusters.

1 PTOLEMY CLUSTER (M7)

This cluster of stars, named after an astronomer from Alexandria (in modern day Egypt), covers a stretch of sky twice the width of the Moon. With the naked eye the cluster appears as a fuzzy patch. Binoculars reveal dozens of bright, blueish stars.

2 ANTARES

Scorpius' brightest star, the heart of the constellation, is the red supergiant Antares. It has a diameter hundreds of times greater than that of our Sun. Antares is Greek for "rival of Mars." It got its name because of its similar hue to the Red Planet.

STORY OF THE STARS

Scorpius is said to be the scorpion that stung and killed Orion the Hunter (page 52). It is one of the 12 zodiac signs that crosses the night sky through the year.

BEST VIEWED
Northern Hemisphere: July–August
Southern Hemisphere: May–September

TAURUS

Easy to find as a V-shape in northern skies, Taurus the Bull charges toward Orion in a battle of the constellations. Taurus contains the remains of an ancient supernova and two major star clusters, the Hyades and the Pleiades.

Aldebaran

1 CRAB NEBULA (M1)
In the year 1054, Chinese astronomers recorded a bright star that suddenly appeared in the sky and stayed visible in the daytime. This has been identified as a supernova, the remains of which can still be seen today as filaments of gas surrounding a neutron star. Through a small telescope the Crab Nebula appears as an oval of gas.

STORY OF THE STARS

This constellation has been identified as a bull for over 5,000 years. The ancient Greeks saw the bull as one of the god Zeus (Jupiter)'s many disguises, one he used to lure the princess Europa before transporting her to the island Crete.

BEST VIEWED
Northern Hemisphere: September–March
Southern Hemisphere: November–February

ALDEBARAN

Taurus' brightest star, Aldebaran, forms the eye of Taurus. This red giant may appear to be part of the Hyades cluster, but it is much closer—only 65 light years away from Earth.

2 THE HYADES

The Hyades are a large cluster of stars and the brightest of them form the head of Taurus. The Hyades are 150 light years away, which is 290 light years closer than the Pleiades!

3 THE PLEIADES (M45)

On Taurus' shoulder is the night sky's most famous and visible cluster, the Pleiades. Though the cluster is often called the Seven Sisters, you may only see six stars, even on a clear night. There are nine named stars in the cluster (the sisters and their parents) though through a telescope you'll see more than 500.

STORY OF THE STARS

The Pleiades were seven nymphs of Greek myth who called to the god Zeus for help when they were pursed by Orion (page 52). Zeus kept them safe by turning them into doves and placing them in the sky.

URSA MAJOR

The northern constellation Ursa Major is widely known for its asterism the Big Dipper (also known as the Plough). It serves as a guide to the Pole Star and features many treasures, including a prominent double star, spiral galaxies, and a birdlike nebula.

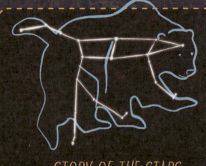

STORY OF THE STARS

One of the earliest identified constellations in Greek mythology, the Great Bear was the nymph Callisto, who was turned into a bear by the goddess Hera as a punishment.

1 MIZAR AND ALCOR

The second star on the Big Dipper's handle is actually a pair, Mizar plus the fainter Alcor. In ancient Rome, soldiers could only beome archers if they could see these as two different stars. With a small telescope, you may see that Mizar is also a binary star.

2 BODE'S GALAXY (M81) AND CIGAR GALAXY (M82)

Visible through binoculars above the neck of the Great Bear, is the bright spiral Bode's Galaxy, named after the German astronomer Johann Elert Bode, who located it in 1774. You'll need a telescope to pick out its fainter neighbor, the Cigar Galaxy (M82). This is a starburst galaxy, with much star-forming activity.

3 OWL NEBULA (M97)

The Owl Nebula was named for its appearance with two large dark patches like eyes. You will need a large telescope to see any detail on this faint object, 2,600 light-years from Earth.

BEST VIEWED
Northern Hemisphere: February–May

URSA MINOR

Resembling a smaller version of the Big Dipper, the Little Bear is the companion constellation of Ursa Major (page 58). It contains the North or Pole Star, which has guided sailors for millennia.

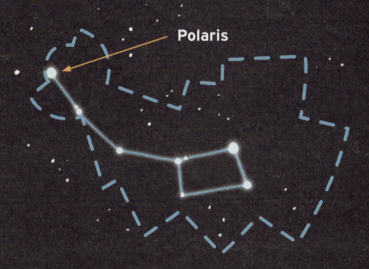

Polaris

THE POLE STAR

Polaris, the northern celestial pole star has been used for centuries as a guide to the direction north, though it is almost one degree away from the position of the actual pole. About 320 light years from Earth, this yellow supergiant has a faint companion star that may be spotted through a small telescope.

STORY OF THE STARS

The Little Bear is said to be a nymph who nursed the infant Greek god Zeus while he was hidden from his murderous father, Cronus. Zeus rewarded the nymph by placing her among the stars.

BEST VIEWED
Northern Hemisphere: May–June

CHAPTER 4: THE SOLAR SYSTEM

From our vantage point on the third of eight planets orbiting the Sun, we have a good view of our neighbors, from the rocky inner planets to the outer gas giants and their many satellites, along with asteroids and passing comets.

The Solar System formed about 4.6 billion years ago, with eight planets and several dwarf planets settling into orbit in almost the same plane around the Sun (which provides the gravitational pull to keep the planets in place). Looking from above the north pole, the planets orbit in a counterclockwise direction.

Counting from the Sun, the Solar System consists of the "rocky planets" Mercury, Venus, Earth, and Mars, followed by a belt of asteroids (rocks that failed to become part of a planet), and the much larger "gas giants," Jupiter, Saturn, Uranus, and Neptune. Beyond Neptune is the Kuiper Belt, home to many large objects including the dwarf planets Pluto and Makemake. Surrounding all of this is the Oort Cloud, home to icy objects including comets which periodically venture within sight of Earth.

Jupiter

Saturn

Uranus

Neptune

*Size and distance are not to scale

THE SUN

Our Sun is an unremarkable yellow dwarf star about halfway through its stable life cycle. It is fueled through nuclear fusion, as hydrogen is converted to helium, releasing vast amounts of light and heat energy.

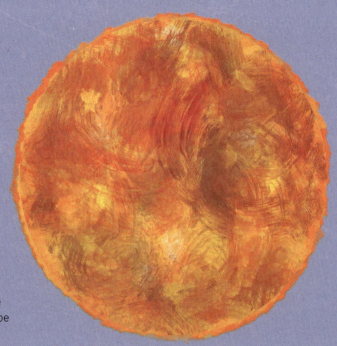

Our closest star is what keeps us alive, providing the light and heat that sustains the perfect environment for us to survive on Earth. Due to its brightness it cannot be observed without extreme precautions.

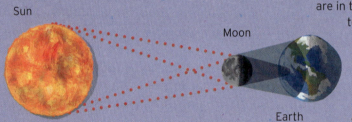

Sun · Moon · Earth

SOLAR ECLIPSES

Roughly twice a year, the Sun, Moon, and Earth are in the right alignment for a partial or total solar eclipse to take place.

Earth's Moon is the perfect size and distance from us (400 times smaller and 400 times closer than the Sun) so that when it passes between our planet and the Sun it completely blots out the star. It takes about 2-3 hours for the Moon to pass in front of the Sun.

A perfect eclipse (totality) is only visible in certain places on Earth in alignment with the Moon and Sun. Outside of this corridor you may see a partial eclipse. With the Sun completely covered for a few minutes, the Sun's corona is revealed. This halo extends for millions of kilometers into space.

SUN FACTS
Diameter 1.39 million km (864,000 mi)
Average distance from Earth 149.6 million km (92.9 million mi)
Volume comparison 1,300,000 Earths
Rotation period 25 Earth days at equator
Surface temperature 5,500°C (9,930°F)

OBSERVING AN ECLIPSE

The Sun should never be observed directly with the naked eye or any unfiltered equipment. Instead, a projection method should be used. Direct your telescope or binocular lens roughly in the direction of the Sun, without looking through the lenses. Point the eyepiece toward a sheet of white card about 50 cm (18 in) away, and move the lenses around until the light of the Sun passes through on to the card. Focus the image using the controls on your telescope or binoculars.

NEVER look directly at the Sun. Doing so can cause permanent damage to your eyesight.

Keep lens cap on finder scope

Fit card sunshade around telescope to improve visibility

The Sun

Keep cards at least 50 cm (18 in) apart

Projection of Sun

Projection of eclipse

Another way to safely view a solar eclipse is by using a pinhole projector, holding a piece of card with a pinhole in its center in front of the Sun. An image of the eclipse should them be projected into the card's shadow.

THE MOON

Earth's satellite is a familiar sight, seen at night and often during the day, with the same face visible from Earth. Through binoculars or a telescope a craggy world of craters and cooled lava lakes opens up.

The only other world in our Solar System to have been visited by humankind, the Moon has been mapped in detail and 4.35 tonnes (4.79 tons) of its rocks collected. The Moon was created four billion years ago when Earth collided with another planet. The huge amount of debris eventually cooled and coalesced to form the Moon.

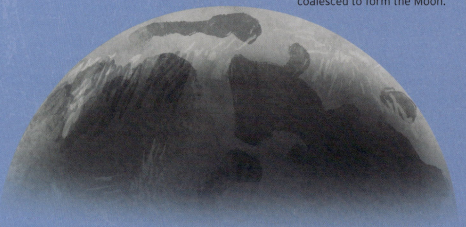

Over time, the rock was compressed by gravity into a sphere, its volcanic activity ended, and its seas of lava cooled. With little of an atmosphere on the Moon, there was nothing to slow down the meteors that were attracted by its gravity and they crashed on to the surface to form large craters. Untouched by wind or rain, these craters have remained intact for billions of years. The footprints of astronauts left 50 years ago will also last.

MOON FACTS
Diameter 3,475 km (2,159 mi)
Average distance from Earth 384,400 km (238,855 mi)
Volume comparison 0.02 Earths
Rotation period 27.3 Earth days
Surface temperature at the equator Day 117 °C (242 °F), Night -178 °C (-288 °F)

PHASES

As Earth and the Moon orbit the Sun, the Moon goes through phases as the Sun's light hits it from a different angle. This cycle lasts 29.5 Earth days, slightly longer than it takes to complete an Earth orbit. As more of the Moon becomes visible it is said to be waxing. As the light disappears, it is waning. When more than half of the Moon is illuminated, the phase is gibbous. These phases present opportunities for astronomers, as new areas are lit up and deeper shadows are cast.

ORBIT

The Moon is in synchronous rotation with Earth. It rotates on its axis over a period of 27.3 Earth days, the same time it takes to orbit Earth, which gives the impression that it does not turn at all. We only see one face of the Moon.

DISTANCE

The Moon's distance from Earth varies over its orbit from 363,300 km (225,744 miles) at lunar perigee (closest point) to 405,500 km (251,966 miles) at lunar apogee (most distant point). The Moon is also slowly moving away from our planet, at a rate of 3.8 cm (1.5 in) a year.

COMPOSITION

The Moon is thought to have a small, mostly iron core surrounded by a 11,190 km (740 miles)-thick rocky mantle. The lunar crust is made of granite-like rock. On the surface, where it has been ground down by meteor collisions, it forms a fine dust called regolith.

OBSERVATION

The best time to view the Moon is during its first or third quarter when sunlight hits the Moon at a low angle and creates strong relief. Mountain ranges and craters are picked out by long shadows. Point your lens toward the terminator, the line between day and night on the Moon, where sunlight ends.

LUNAR HIGHLIGHTS

The near side of the Moon is filled with fascinating sights, including thousands of impact craters, mountain ranges, and smooth "seas," where lava once flowed. Many craters are named after famous astronomers.

THE LUNAR SURFACE

The surface of the Moon is covered with craters and maria (Latin for seas). The craters are the result of numerous collisions from meteors and asteroids, with dust rising then settling a distance from the point of impact. The maria are areas where magma seeped through cracks in the lunar surface. The lava cooled to form relatively smooth plains that appear darker than the higher regions.

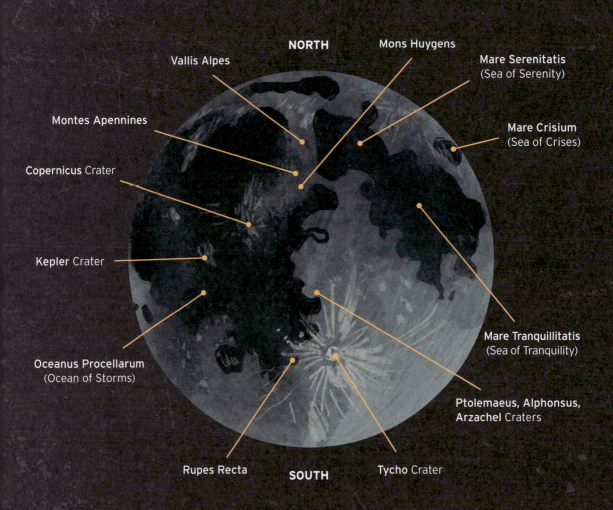

- NORTH
- Vallis Alpes
- Mons Huygens
- Mare Serenitatis (Sea of Serenity)
- Mare Crisium (Sea of Crises)
- Montes Apennines
- Copernicus Crater
- Kepler Crater
- Mare Tranquillitatis (Sea of Tranquility)
- Oceanus Procellarum (Ocean of Storms)
- Ptolemaeus, Alphonsus, Arzachel Craters
- Rupes Recta
- SOUTH
- Tycho Crater

MONTES APENNINES

This lunar mountain range extends for 600 km (370 mi) and includes Mons Huygens, the Moon's highest mountain at 5,500 m (18,046 ft).

PTOLEMAEUS, ALPHONSUS, ARZACHEL

This trio of craters form a north-to-south chain. Ptolemaeus is the largest, at 153 km (95 mi) diameter and positioned almost in the center of the Moon's near face. South of Ptolemaeus is Alphonsus, followed by Arzachel.

COPERNICUS CRATER

This 93 km (58 mi)-wide crater is surrounded by material that was ejected during the initial impact that caused the crater. This material reaches for hundreds of kilometers. Look for peaks in the center of the crater.

RUPES RECTA

The "straight wall" Rupes Recta, is a 110 km (68 mi)-long cliff. The Sun must be lighting the Moon at a low angle for the cliff's shadow to be visible.

TYCHO CRATER

Toward the south pole, Tycho Crater is notable for the rays that extend 1,500 km (930 mi) away from the rim. It is thought the crater formed 108 million years ago, during the age of the dinosaurs.

MARE CRISIUM

Mares Crisium is an almost circular sea, separate from all the others. The edge of its smooth lava field is worth exploring, as it is pockmarked with small craters.

VALLIS ALPES

The Vallis Alpes (Alpine Alley) is a 166 km (103 mi)-long valley in the Montes Alpes. At its widest point it is 10 km across. A large telescope may reveal the thin crack (rille) that divides the valley.

LUNAR ECLIPSES

When the Earth passes between the Sun and the Moon it casts a shadow across the surface of the Moon, causing an eclipse that can last for several minutes. The Moon may then appear a deep red.

MERCURY

The closest planet to the Sun is not much larger than our Moon. Crater-covered Mercury is best seen as a light just above the horizon early or late in the day.

In close proximity to the Sun, Mercury is a planet of extremes. This dry, rocky world has a surface temperature on the Sun-facing side hot enough to melt lead. The side in shadow is as cold as that at Earth's poles. Like our Moon, Mercury is pitted with thousands of craters, where meteors smashed into the young planet, between smooth plains of cooled lava.

OBSERVATION

Not only is Mercury close to the Sun and hidden by its glare, it also races around the star, orbiting four times as fast as Earth. Your best chances of spotting this planet are shortly after sunset in spring (in the northern hemisphere). Mercury will be shining like a star at these times but you'll need to be prepared as it will only remain visible just above the horizon for 45 minutes tops. Through a telescope you may notice that Mercury goes through phases like the Moon and Venus.

MERCURY FACTS
Diameter 4,879 km (3,032 mi)
Average distance from Sun 58 million km (36 million mi)
Volume comparison 0.056 Earths
Moons 0
Rotation period 59 Earth days
Surface temperature -180°C (-292°F) to 430°C (806°F)

VENUS

At times, Venus is the closest planet to our own and the brightest in our sky. While named for the Roman goddess of love, this planet is a boiling hot danger zone with crushing pressures and acid rains.

Venus is the second-closest planet to the Sun but it's the hottest due to its thick carbon dioxide atmosphere that traps heat. Its clouds contain sulfuric acid and the atmospheric pressure near the surface is 92 times that of Earth. Space probes have lasted just hours on its hellish surface. The planet has endured much volcanic activity with vast lava lakes covering 85% of its low-lying plains. Its largest peak is Skadi Mons, which rises to 11 km (7 mi) above the surface.

Venus rotates in the opposite direction to the other planets in the Solar System. It also rotates very slowly, with one day on Venus equal to 243 Earth days, longer than a Venusian year (225 Earth days).

OBSERVATION

From Earth, Venus appears as a bland gray-blue disk. Regular telescopes can't penetrate its cloud. The planet is commonly visible for hours early and late in the day, which is why it gained the names Morning Star and Evening Star. Sunlight reflects well off its pale clouds, making it the third brightest stellar object in our sky after the Sun and Moon, at its maximum apparent magnitude of -4.6.

Venus goes through phases like our Moon as it orbits the Sun. It is closest to Earth during its crescent phase and appears at its brightest to us then. While the Moon takes a month to complete its cycle of phases, Venus takes about 584 days!

VENUS FACTS

Diameter 12,104 km (7,520 mi)
Average distance from Sun 108 million km (67 million mi)
Volume comparison 0.86 Earths
Moons 0
Rotation period 243 Earth days
Surface temperature 464°C (867°F)

MARS

Images of Mars are beamed to us daily from rovers exploring its surface but the Red Planet has lost none of its fascination. Its rusty hue is easy to pick out against the stars.

Mars has a surface area similar in size to the land masses of Earth but it is a cold desert of iron-rich rock and dust (hence its rusty color). Liquid water cannot last long below its thin atmosphere but there is evidence it once followed channels across the surface. Water ice is held at its poles, however, something of vital importance for any future human missions to the planet.

Mars is a planet of highs and lows. Its 4,000 km (2,500 mi)-long Valles Marineris canyons are 8 km (5 mi) deep in parts. The volcano Olympus Mons is the highest mountain in the Solar System, 22 km (13.7 mi) high, over twice the height of Mount Everest. The volcano may still be active.

OBSERVATION

Mars' eccentric orbit means it can be anywhere between 56 million km (35 million mi) and 400 million km (250 million mi) from Earth. It shines red in the night sky and is brightest in opposition, when it is at its closest, every two years or so. Depending on the planet's angle and spin, through a telescope, you may see patterns on the surface, such as the black volcanic rocks of Syrtis Major Planum and Solis Lacus (Eye of Mars), or the white of polar ice. Such sightings can be spoilt, however, by the planet's frequent dust storms, some of which sweep across the whole planet.

MARS FACTS
Diameter 6,779 km (4,212 mi)
Average distance from Sun 228 million km (142 million mi)
Volume comparison 0.15 Earths
Moons 2
Rotation period 24.6 Earth hours
Surface temperature 27°C (80.6°F) daytime to -133°C nighttime (-207.4°F)

MARS' MOONS

Mars has two irregular-shaped moons, Phobos and Deimos, but these are far too small to be seen through a small telescope. The larger, Phobos, is only 26 km (16 mi) across at its widest point.

MARS MISSIONS

More missions have been sent to Mars than to any other planet in the Solar System, over 40 in total. These include numerous probes and several robot explorers that have rolled across the surface, sharing photos and investigating rock samples. Many remain in orbit while robots, including the *Perseverance* rover, scour the surface. *Perseverance* is collecting and storing soil samples for collection in the 2030s.

A human mission to Mars has been proposed for decades. The mission would require astronauts to spend nine months in transit then about 16 months in bases on the ground before a return—34 months in total. No date has been fixed for such a mission.

JUPITER

The largest planet in the Solar System is a gas giant with a mass several times greater than all the other planets combined. Jupiter's atmosphere is a swirling pattern of storms, including the Great Red Spot.

Jupiter has a rocky core with an atmosphere of mostly hydrogen and helium thousands of kilometers deep. The planet's fast rotational speed churns the cloud layer to create vast swirling storms. The Great Red Spot is just one of many visible on the surface. At about 16,350 km (10,159 mi) across, it could swallow the Earth. Historical sightings record it being several times larger and suggest it has been spinning for over 200 years.

Jupiter's great mass keeps almost a hundred moons in its orbit and it deflects the passage of nearby asteroids and comets. It also helps prevent a planet forming from the asteroids in the asteroid belt.

JUPITER FACTS
Diameter 142,984 km (88,846 mi)
Average distance from Sun 778 million km (484 million mi)
Volume comparison 1,321 Earths
Moons 95
Rotation period 9.93 Earth hours
Cloud-top temperature -145°C (-234°F)

OBSERVATION

Jupiter appears in opposition and at its brightest every 13 months and remains high in the sky for most of the night. Through a telescope, you should be able to make out Jupiter as a slightly squashed disk with its four Galilean moons. Jupiter bulges at its equator due to its fast spin—a Jupiter day is just 10 Earth hours. You may also see a few colored bands of cloud around the equator, and perhaps even the Great Red Spot in its southern hemisphere. Due to the wild weather on Jupiter, its appearance changes often. With a large telescope you may occasionally see transit shadows from the largest moons on Jupiter's surface.

GALILEAN MOONS

In 1610, with the aid of a telescope, the Italian astronomer Galileo Galilei spied four moons orbiting Jupiter, supporting the controversial idea that Earth revolved around the Sun, rather the opposite. The four moons described by Galileo—Io, Europa, Ganymede, and Callisto—can all be seen through binoculars or a small telescope, in a vaguely straight line. Ganymede is larger than the planet Mercury.

Europa's ice covering may hide liquid water, making it one of the few worlds in the Solar System, outside of Earth, where life may be detected. More powerful telescopes and detection methods have discovered many more satellites around Jupiter since Galileo's time, with 95 accepted at the time of writing.

SATURN

Saturn is one of the most compelling sights for a new astronomer. The gas giant is smaller and twice as far from Earth as Jupiter but large enough to appear like a bright star in the night sky thanks to its magnificent, reflective rings.

Saturn is a gas giant like Jupiter but even less dense. It would float in water. The planet is mostly composed of hydrogen and helium, as a gas at the surface then as liquid and liquid metal toward the center, as the temperature and pressure increases. Saturn has a short day of under 11 Earth hours. Its spin helps generate storms in the upper atmosphere. Around the equator winds can race at 1,800 km/h (1,100 mph).

Saturn has more moons than any other planet in the Solar System. These are mostly made up of rock and ice. The largest of Saturn's satellites is Titan which, at 5,150 km (3,200 mi) in diameter, is about the same size as the planet Mercury (page 68). Titan also has its own atmosphere of nitrogen and methane.

OBSERVATION

Saturn can be seen in the night sky for about 10 months of the year. It remains in bright opposition for about two weeks. Its rings are visible with an average-sized telescope. As the planet is tilted during its orbit of the Sun, you may see the rings at different angles—sometimes side on, as a thin line dividing the planet in two, or from above or below, as a wide band. The rings reflect sunlight well, making them easy to see from a great distance. With a large telescope you may see some banding on the planet, a divide in the ring system, and even some of Saturn's larger moons dotted around the planet.

THE RINGS

Saturn's ring system extends over 282,000 km (175,000 mi) from the planet but it is only a few meters thick. The rings are mostly composed of boulders and dust made of dirty water ice, likely to be the remains of moons. The clear gap that splits the ring system in two is called the Cassini Division. Beyond the familiar rings that circle the planet, there are fainter sets including one tilted at a different angle and located as far as 12 million km (7.4 million mi) away from Saturn.

SATURN FACTS

Diameter 120,536 km (74,898 mi)

Average distance from Sun 1.45 billion km (886 billion mi)

Volume comparison 764 Earths

Moons 146

Rotation period 10.67 Earth hours

Cloud-top temperature -139°C (-218°F)

URANUS

Uranus was the first planet to be discovered through a telescope, in 1781. This blue icy giant is unique in the Solar System for rotating on its side rather than in line with its solar orbit.

Uranus is a large, cold planet, about four times the size of Earth, with an atmosphere consisting mostly of hydrogen and helium. Its blue color is the result of methane ice in the atmosphere absorbing the red parts of the light spectrum. Uranus' axis of rotation is almost at a right angle to the plane of its orbit of the Sun. This may be the result of some ancient collision. The tilt of the planet means that for a quarter of its year, sunlight only hits the poles, throwing the rest of the planet into a 21-year-long winter. Temperatures here are the lowest for any planet In the Solar System with the coldest recorded at -224°C (-371°F).

In line with its titled axis, Uranus also has a very faint system of 13 rings, separated by wide gaps.

URANUS FACTS
Diameter 51,118 km (31,763 mi)
Average distance from Sun 2.9 billion km (1.8 billion mi)
Volume comparison 63 Earths
Moons 28
Rotation period 17.24 Earth hours
Cloud-top temperature -197°C (-323°F)

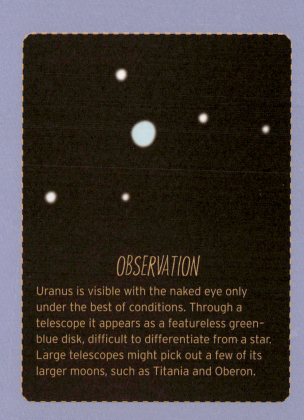

OBSERVATION

Uranus is visible with the naked eye only under the best of conditions. Through a telescope it appears as a featureless green-blue disk, difficult to differentiate from a star. Large telescopes might pick out a few of its larger moons, such as Titania and Oberon.

NEPTUNE

The most distant planet from the Sun in our Solar System, Neptune was only discovered in 1846. This deep-blue world with savage storms presents a challenge for astronomers seeking it against a starry sky.

OBSERVATION

Neptune is too far away to be seen without lenses. Binoculars or a small telescope should pick it out when the planet reaches its maximum magnitude of 7.7, though you will need a clear guide as to where to look. A large telescope, 150 mm (6 in) or more, is needed to show Neptune as a simple blue disk along with its largest moon, Triton.

Little was known of distant Neptune until 1989, when the space probe Voyager 2 passed by. We now understand it to be a rich blue planet with a hydrogen atmosphere wracked by storms. The fastest winds in the Solar System have been recorded here, up to 2,100 km/h (1,300 mph). For periods, large dark storm clouds appear in the upper atmosphere, similar to Jupiter's Great Red Spot. Beneath the clouds is icy water, methane, and ammonia, surrounding a small, rocky core. Neptune is a similar size to Uranus. Its blue hue comes from small amounts of methane in the atmosphere. Neptune has a faint system of five rings that may be comprised of ice particles.

NEPTUNE FACTS
Diameter 49,528 km (30,775 mi)
Average distance from Sun 4.5 billion km (2.8 billion mi)
Volume comparison 57.7 Earths
Moons 16
Rotation period 16.11 Earth hours
Cloud-top temperature -200°C (-328°F)

DWARF PLANETS

In 2006, Pluto was relegated to dwarf planet status, a position it shares with four other official minor solar satellites. While these rocks are small and distant it is possible to locate a few through a telescope.

For 76 years, following its discovery in 1930, Pluto was listed as one of nine planets in the Solar System. It was a faraway dot about half the width of the United States, smaller than seven planetary moons including our own. Little surface detail was seen through the telescopes of the time. Following its demotion, thanks to the space probe New Horizons that passed it by in 2015, Pluto has been revealed as a handsome cratered and rocky world with an icy mantle and crust plus an atmosphere containing nitrogen, carbon monoxide, and methane. Pluto also has five tiny moons in its orbit.

OBSERVATION

Through a telescope the dwarf planets look indistinguishable from stars and they pose a challenge to find. You will need an app or up-to-date guide to find out which constellations they are passing through and when before scouring the heavens. Ceres, the closest, may be seen through binoculars. For Pluto you will need a telescope 200 mm (8 in) or larger.

WHAT MAKES A DWARF PLANET?

The definition of a dwarf planet is that of a body in orbit around the Sun with enough mass and gravity to give it a mostly spherical shape but one that has not cleared its orbital path of other materials.

There are five officially accepted dwarf planets. Pluto, Eris, Haumea, and Makemake are all found beyond Neptune, in and around the Kuiper Belt (page 79). Ceres, the smallest of the five, is the largest body in the Asteroid Belt between Mars and Jupiter. Many other potential dwarf planets have been discovered, awaiting official recognition.

PLUTO FACTS
Diameter 2,376 km (1,476 mi)
Average distance from Sun 5.9 billion km (3.7 billion mi)
Volume comparison 0.006 Earths
Moons 5
Rotation period 6.39 Earth days
Cloud-top temperature -240°C (-400°F)

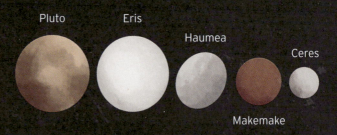

Pluto Eris Haumea Ceres Makemake

78

KUIPER BELT AND BEYOND

Just outside the orbit of Neptune is the Kuiper Belt, a flattened expanse of icy bodies, including dwarf planets. Beyond this is the spherical Oort Cloud. These dark, outer regions are the source of comets that periodically pass in sighting distance from Earth.

The Kuiper Belt, named after the Dutch astronomer Gerard Kuiper, is a thick disk of small icy bodies. It comprises leftover debris from the birth of the Solar System, orbiting the Sun between 4.5 and 7.5 billion km (2.8 and 4.6 billion mi) away, outside the orbit of Neptune. The dwarf planets Pluto and Eris travel within this region.

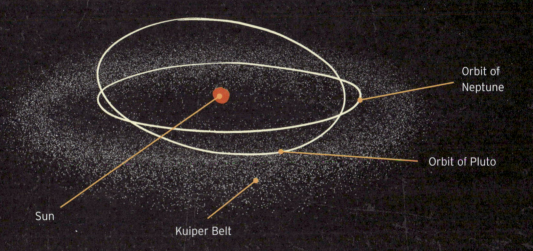

Orbit of Neptune
Orbit of Pluto
Sun
Kuiper Belt

THE OORT CLOUD

Bordering the Kuiper Belt and surrounding the planets of the Solar System is thought to be a spherical shell about 1.6 light years in diameter. It lies about a fifth of the distance from the Sun to the next-nearest star, Proxima Centauri (page 45). The cloud contains trillions of icy comet-like objects (page 80). The gravitational influence of nearby stars may, on occasion, nudge these objects to leave the cloud and enter the Solar System as comets.

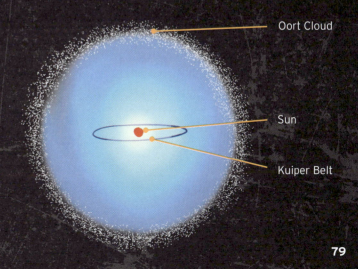

Oort Cloud
Sun
Kuiper Belt

COMETS

Comets are dirty balls of ice that leave the outer reaches of the Solar System on a journey that may take millions of years. On occasions they pass within sight of Earth, providing an attractive target for astronomers.

Comets begin as nuclei of ice and dust in the Kuiper Belt or Oort Cloud (page 79). These nuclei can be a few hundred meters to tens of kilometers across. At some point a nuclei may be drawn into a new elliptical orbit around the Sun.

Those from the Kuiper Belt are short-period comets with an orbit which lasts less than 200 years. The famous Halley's Comet is one example. This orbits the Sun every 76 years and is next due in sight of Earth in 2061. Those from the Oort Cloud are long-period comets and may be seen just once in a human lifetime as their complete circuit may take thousands, even millions of years.

As comets move close to the Sun, they are affected by the Sun's heat and some of their material is vaporized to form two tails, one of dust and the other of gases. The tails are directed away from the star by solar wind and radiation. A comet's tail may measure millions of kilometers in length. If Earth passes through the dust left behind by a comet, the dust may fall to Earth as a meteor shower (page 82).

Almost 5,000 comets have been recorded by astronomers. Roughly one comet visible to the unaided eye passes close enough to Earth each year. The comet Hale-Bopp was clear to see in the night sky when it passed within 197 million km (122 million mi) of Earth in 1997. This bright comet is not due to pass by again for another 2,400 years. Follow astronomy websites to find out when the next visible comets are expected.

ASTEROIDS

Asteroids are chunks of rock and metal left over from the formation of the Solar System 4.6 billion years ago. Most lie in a belt between Mars and Jupiter.

In a wide ring between the planets Mars and Jupiter lies the Main Belt, home to 90% of the asteroids in the Solar System. There are millions of these rocks in orbit around the Sun. The largest among them is the dwarf planet Ceres (page 78). At 952 km (592 mi) in diameter, it is a quarter the size of our Moon. Most asteroids are irregular in shape and range in size from hundreds of kilometers across to the size of a pebble. There are hundreds of thousands of kilometers between asteroids in the belt.

Some asteroids, known as near-Earth asteroids, have orbits outside of the belt while others named trojans follow Jupiter's orbit (or the orbit of another planet). Occasionally asteroids collide. Their fragments may be directed toward Earth and fall as meteors (page 82).

ASTEROID COLLECTION

In 2016, the van-sized space probe OSIRIS-REx was launched from Earth toward the space rock Bennu where it gathered samples of the near-Earth asteroid's material four years later. These fragments were safely delivered by capsule to Earth in 2023 where they can be studied by scientists and provide information on the early conditions of the Solar System. OSIRIS-REx is now headed toward a second asteroid, Apophis, between Earth and Mars, which it is expected to orbit in 2029.

METEORS

When pieces of asteroids and comets pass through Earth's atmosphere they burn up as they fall and appear as meteors or "shooting stars" in the sky.

As Earth orbits the Sun it passes through areas of space where the debris of asteroids and comets remains. Pulled in by Earth's gravity, these lumps of rock and metal, often the size of dust particles, burn up as they descend through the atmosphere at speeds of around 20 km (12 mi) per second. These meteors, commonly known as "shooting stars," light up the sky with their short-lived, bright trails. Millions of meteors, usually the size of grains of sand, are incinerated in Earth's atmosphere daily at an altitude of 80 km (50 mi) or higher.

METEORITES

When a meteor is large enough (above 30 kg/66 lb) and survives to land on the ground it is called a meteorite. An estimated 44 tonnes (49 tons) of meteoritic material lands on Earth every day. Meteorites are typically made up of stone, iron, and nickel.

In the past, Earth has been hit by giant meteors which left craters on the surface. One, which hit the Yucatán Peninsula in Mexico 66 million years ago, resulted in a massive blast wave, tidal waves, and a layer of soot that blocked out much of the Sun's light and caused the death of plants and non-avian dinosaurs. Thankfully, such mammoth meteors are extremely rare. Any near-Earth objects that threaten a close approach are tracked by ground telescopes.

Barringer Crater, Arizona, USA

METEOR SHOWERS

Highlights of the year for many astronomers are the annual meteor showers when Earth passes through a significant area of comet debris. This results in a steady stream of shooting stars called meteor showers. They are named after the constellations they appear to emerge from.

THE BEST OF THE ANNUAL METEOR SHOWERS ARE:

MONTH	METEOR SHOWER	SOURCE
May	Eta Aquariids	Aquarius (page 36)
August	Perseids	Perseus
October	Orionids	Orion (page 52)
November	Leonids	Leo (page 36)
December	Geminids	Gemini (page 36)

CHAPTER 5: DEEP SKY

Perhaps the greatest appeal of astronomy is locating the most distant treasures in the night sky, the deep-sky objects. These include large gaseous clouds called nebulae where new stars are born, galaxies like or unlike our own, and the variety of stars from white dwarfs to red supergiants alone, paired or in sparkling clusters.

What distant wonders
will you discover?

STARS

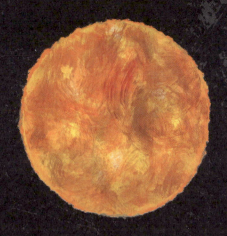

Stars are huge, dynamic balls of hydrogen and helium gas, heated to incredible levels through the process of nuclear fusion (page 86). Their huge masses generate the gravity that keeps them together and binds planetary systems. The energy they release provides the warmth to sustain life and lights the Universe.

Though the stars are light years distant, with the naked eye it is possible to see differences between them. Some are obviously brighter than others. This may be due to their closeness to Earth, their age, or volume. Some have a red, an orange, or a blue hue. This is due to their surface temperature. Every star is different.

STAR CLASSIFICATION

Stars are classified according to their spectra—the wavelengths of light they emit. The classification system goes from the hottest, blue O-type stars to the coolest, red M-type stars. Our Sun is a G-type star, with a surface temperature of about 5,500 °C (9,900 °F).

MAXIMUM SURFACE TEMPERATURE FOR EACH STAR TYPE

O	B	A	F	G	K	M
Over 24,726 °C	9,726°C	7,226°C	5,726°C	4,726°C	3,226°C	Under 3,226 °C
Over 44,540°F	17,540°F	13,040°F	10,340°F	8,540°F	5,840°F	Under 5,840 °F

LIFE OF A STAR

Stars are made of hydrogen and helium gas undergoing a nuclear reaction that releases energy as light and heat. They are born within vast clouds of gas but they may develop and end their lives in different, sometimes explosive ways.

BIRTH OF A STAR

Stars form in space when clouds of dust and gas are brought together and collapse under their own gravity. As the gas becomes denser, the core heats up, and the ball of gas starts spinning. More material is drawn into this protostar, its mass and temperature increase further and the protostar begins to glow. Eventually it reaches a point when nuclear fusion can begin.

Nuclear fusion is when two nuclei of hydrogen atoms, the lightest element, combine to form the nuclei of the next heaviest element, helium. During this process energy is released, radiating from the star into space. While hot matter and radiation push outward from the star, gravity holds the star together in a balancing act which can last for millions or billions of years.

STAR EVOLUTION

Stars that remain stable, generating energy for millions of years, are called main-sequence stars. What happens in their life cycle, when their fuel runs low, depends on their mass. As the hydrogen in the star's core is used up, gas in the outer levels is burnt. The star cools and expands.

A star with a low mass will cool and shrink to become a dim and cold black dwarf.

A medium star, like our Sun, may expand into a red giant. Its outer layers become a cloud of gas and dust called a planetary nebula (page 92) as the star collapses to become a white dwarf.

A high-mass star may grow into a supergiant and explode as a supernova, leaving behind a super-dense neutron star or black hole with an enormous gravitational pull.

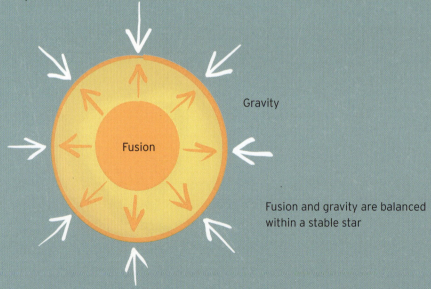

Fusion and gravity are balanced within a stable star

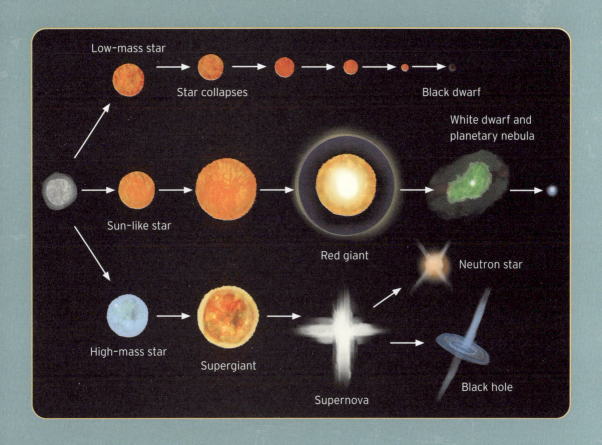

GIANT SPOTTING

There are several giant stars worth seeking in the night sky. Here's where to find them:

Star type	Name	Constellation
Red supergiant	Betelgeuse	Orion (page 52)
Red supergiant	Antares	Scorpius (page 55)
Red giant	Aldebaran	Taurus (page 56)
Blue supergiant	Eta Carinae	Carina (page 43)
Red giant	Pollux	Gemini (page 36)

MULTIPLE AND VARIABLE STARS

Stars in various combinations provide interesting targets for astronomers, whether as multiple star systems, variable stars, or glittering global clusters.

BINARY AND MULTIPLE STARS

Binary and multiple star systems occur when stars are created from the same mass of cloud and dust and are held together by gravity. The connected stars do not necessarily develop in the same way, so mixed pairings are common, with one star larger than the other.

MULTIPLE STARS TO FIND

STAR TYPE	NAME	CONSTELLATION
Binary	Albireo	Cygnus (page 47)
Binary	Sirius	Canis Major (page 42)
Multiple	Epsilon Lyrae	Lyra (page 51)
Multiple	Mizar	Ursa Major (page 58)

VARIABLE STARS TO FIND

TYPE	NAME	CONSTELLATION
Pulsating variable	Delta Cephei	Cepheus
Pulsating variable	Betelgeuse	Orion (page 52)
Pulsating variable	Mekbuda	Gemini (page 36)
Eclipsing binary	Algol	Perseus
Eclipsing binary	Beta Lyrae	Lyra (page 51)

VARIABLE STARS

Some stars change their level of brightness over time, over hours or years. There are two kinds to look for. Intrinsic variable stars pulsate or vary their brightness in a cycle. Extrinsic variable stars have their light affected by an external source such as a binary partner passing in front of it.

CLUSTERS

Clusters may include a dozen or several million stars all held together by gravity. They may contain stars that were born at the same time from the same source.

There are two types of cluster to seek out. Open clusters are relatively young, with fewer stars loosely connected. Globular clusters are larger groups usually arranged in a sphere and more concentrated toward the center.

CLUSTERS TO FIND

TYPE	NAME	CONSTELLATION
Open	Pleiades (M45)	Taurus (page 56)
Open	Hyades	Taurus (page 56)
Open	Jewel Box	Crux (page 46)
Open	Butterfly Cluster (M6)	Scorpius (page 55)
Globular	Omega Centauri	Centaurus (page 45)
Globular	Great Globular Cluster (M13)	Hercules (page 49)

GALAXIES

The existence of other galaxies beyond our own Milky Way was only established about 100 years ago. We now know there are billions of them, with many hundreds to be seen through a small telescope.

Galaxies are huge systems containing billions of stars and planets, dust and gas clouds. They are held together by gravity and likely to have a giant black hole at the center. There are several types of galaxies. Most have spiral shapes like our own Milky Way (page 20) while the rest form ovals or irregular patterns.

The Pinwheel Galaxy

SPIRAL GALAXIES

Spiral galaxies appear as rotating disks with several arms curving outward from a bulging center. The arms appear bright as these are where young blue and white stars are being born. The center contains older red and yellow stars. Barred spirals have a wider, less spherical central bulge, with arms stretching from each end.

LENTICULAR GALAXIES

These lens-shaped galaxies have a bulging center surrounded by a disk but do not have the arms of a spiral galaxy.

ELLIPTICAL GALAXIES

Elliptical galaxies are bound in a stretched ball or cigar shape. They contain less gas and fewer new stars than spiral galaxies and are made up of mostly old red and yellow stars.

IRREGULAR GALAXIES

Irregular galaxies may have developed their haphazard shapes due to a cosmic collision.

Elliptical

Spiral

Barred spiral

Irregular

Lenticular

GALAXIES TO FIND

Here are a few of the best and brightest galaxies to track down.

TYPE	NAME	CONSTELLATION
Spiral	Andromeda Galaxy (M31)	Andromeda (page 40)
Spiral	Triangulum Galaxy (M33)	Triangulum (page 40)
Spiral	Pinwheel Galaxy (M101)	Ursa Major (page 58)
Spiral	Bodes Galaxy (M81)	Ursa Major (page 58)
Spiral	Cigar Galaxy (M82)	Ursa Major (page 58)
Spiral	Sombrero Galaxy (M104)	Virgo (page 36)
Elliptical	M87 (and Virgo Cluster)	Virgo (page 36)

NEBULAE

Nebulae are enormous clouds of gas and dust, often hundreds of light years across, and both the beginning and end for stars. They may be the debris of supernovae or the nurseries for a new generation of stars. They provide some of the most picturesque sights in the heavens.

PLANETARY NEBULAE

Planetary nebula have nothing to do with planets but are the result of a dying red giant star losing its outer shell of gas (page 86). These nebulae may appear as huge smoke rings or swirls of gas. Their various shapes have led to them receiving descriptive names such as the Owl, Eagle, or Dumbbell Nebula. Pushed around by external forces, these clouds of gas may become compressed by gravity and begin the process of developing new stars.

The Eagle Nebula

NEBULAE TO FIND

Here are a few of the most spectacular nebulae to track down. Most will appear gray through binoculars or a telescope. To see a range of pinks and other colors, you will need to take a long-exposure photograph (page 31).

Emission nebulae and planetary nebulae emit their own light. Reflection nebulae reflect the light from neighboring stars. Dark nebulae, such as the Horsehead Nebula in Orion (page 52), give off no light and are seen as dark patches against the stars.

NEBULA TYPE	NAME	CONSTELLATION
Emission	Orion Nebula (M42)	Orion (page 52)
Emission	Carina Nebula (M51)	Carina (page 43)
Planetary	Ring Nebula (M57)	Lyra (page 51)
Supernova remnant	Crab Nebula (M1)	Taurus (page 56)
Planetary	Dumbbell Nebula (M27)	Vulpecula
Planetary	North American Nebula	Cygnus (page 47)
Emission	Lagoon Nebula (M8)	Sagittarius (page 54)

SUPERNOVA REMNANTS

Nebulae are sometimes the result of a cataclysmic explosion called a supernova. This was the case for the Crab Nebula (page 56) which was witnessed as a bright light in the sky by astronomers in the eleventh century.

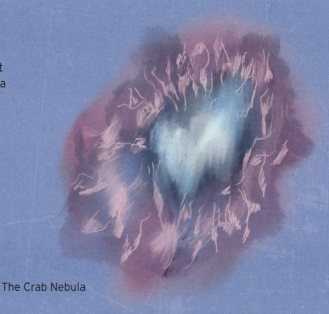

The Crab Nebula

93

TAKING IT FURTHER

Once you're hooked on astronomy you may want to expand your night-time horizons by joining a group or visiting observatories and dark-sky reserves.

VISITING OBSERVATORIES

Many large observatories offer opportunities for visitors to study the skies through the largest of telescopes. Some also put on courses for beginner astronomers.

JOINING CLUBS

Astronomy does not have to be a solo activity. There are many local and national amateur astronomy societies that meet regularly to stargaze and be involved in presentations on astronomical topics. Joining a group is a great way to make friends with fellow stargazers, gain experience, share observations, and try out new equipment. Look online for your nearest club.

DARK-SKY RESERVES

For the best stargazing conditions, you need to visit what is called a dark-sky reserve. These places, designated by the Dark-Sky Association, are generally well away from the artificial lights of towns and cities and provide the best conditions for stargazing, as long as the weather allows. You should be able to enjoy fine views of the Milky Way in these locations.

If you choose to visit one of these sites, do check the weather forecast to avoid cloud, and the lunar calendar to avoid a bright Moon. Also, use a red flashlight for finding your way without spoiling your night vision.

With so many options and locations, and so many sights and astronomical events to look forward to, stargazing truly is an activity without limit.

GLOSSARY

Accretion disk - a flattened ring of material formed when it is pulled toward a powerful gravitational force, such as a black hole

Altazimuth - a telescopic mount that moves at an angle above the horizon (altitude) and east or west (azimuth)

Altitude - height above sea or ground level

Apogee - the point in the Moon or a satellite's orbit when it is farthest from Earth

Asterism - a pattern of bright stars usually smaller than a constellation

Axis - an imaginary line between a planet's poles around which it spins

Azimuth - angle of an object east or west measured clockwise from 0° north

Celestial pole - most northerly or southerly point on the celestial sphere

Celestial sphere - an imaginary sphere with Earth at the center and the stars and planets mapped over its surface

Celestial meridian - an imaginary line that passes through the celestial poles and the zenith (a point directly above the viewer)

Conjunction - an alignment of planets or other celestial bodies that makes them appear close to each other

Constellation - one of 88 patterns of stars within a fixed boundary

Declination - angle of an object north or south of the celestial equator

Dwarf planet - a spherical body that does not clear its orbital path around the Sun

Eclipse - event when three celestial bodies line up so the middle object blocks the light from the body behind

Ecliptic - the Sun's apparent path across Earth's sky over a year

Electromagnetic spectrum - the range of electromagnetic radiation types, which includes radio waves, infrared, visible light, ultraviolet, X-rays, and gamma rays

Equatorial - a telescopic mount that is set up in line with the equator of the celestial sphere

Equinox - the date when the Sun crosses the celestial equator and Earth's day and night are of equal length

Gibbous - (of the Moon) more than half but less than fully illuminated

Hemisphere - half of a sphere, usually divided into northern and southern halves

Latitude - position in degrees north or south of the equator

Light pollution - brightening of the night sky caused by artificial lights

Light year - the distance that light (the fastest thing in the Universe) travels in one year, equal to 9.5 trillion km (5.9 trillion mi)

Longitude - position in degrees east or west of the prime or celestial meridian

Magnitude - a measure of the brightness of a star or celestial body

Mantle - a region of a planet's interior between its crust and core

Mare - a large, level plain on the Moon. (Plural: maria)

Objective lens - the lens in an optical device nearest to the object being viewed

Opposition - the position of a planet or celestial body in the opposite direction to the Sun, as seen from Earth

Perigee - the point in a satellite's orbit when it is closest to Earth

Protostar - a mass of compressed gas in the early stages of becoming a star, before nuclear fusion begins

Regolith - a layer of loose material covering solid rock

Retrograde - an apparent reverse direction for a planet as viewed from Earth, due to relative orbital motion

Solstice - the date when the Sun reaches its maximum declination and Earth's day or night is at its maximum length

Spectra - a range of electromagnetic wavelengths emitted by an object, such as a star

Transit - the passing of one celestial body in front of another, larger one

Vernal equinox - the equinox in March when the Sun crosses the celestial equator in a northerly direction. Also called First Point of Aries

Waning - the period in a Moon's phases when its illuminated part decreases

Waxing - the period in a Moon's phases when its illuminated part increases

Zenith - a point directly above the viewer, at right angles to the ground

Zodiac - a group of 13 constellations which the Sun passes through over the year